UNCOVERING SPIRITUAL NARRATIVES

UNCOVERING SPIRITUAL NARRATIVES

USING STORY IN PASTORAL CARE AND MINISTRY

SUZANNE M. COYLE

Fortress Press
Minneapolis

UNCOVERING SPIRITUAL NARRATIVES

Using Story in Pastoral Care and Ministry

Material in chapters 1 and 5 has been adapted from the author's 2013 publication, *Re-Storying Your Faith* (Circle Books). Used with Permission.

Cover Image: © Thinkstock

Cover design: Erica Rieck

Library of Congress Cataloging-in-Publication Data

Print ISBN: 978-0-8006-9929-1

eBook ISBN: 978-1-4514-3868-0

Manufactured in the U.S.A.

This book was produced using PressBooks.com, and PDF rendering was done by PrinceXML.

For

My husband Peter and son Joel

Main characters in my life story

CONTENTS

PREFACE

"Books are your friends," my mother told me as she read to me from the Bible storybook and the Childcraft books. They held stories that, as an only child, I embraced and cherished as my friends. Such has been my fascination with stories. I love listening to and telling stories. I love reading stories. So, imagine my joy when I discovered narrative therapy that honored stories to enrich personal identity.

I knew that just honoring stories of any variety, however, was not enough. I delight now in my journey to tell stories of life along with stories of faith, to extend the storytelling to ministers, students, and scholars.

This book strives to offer a theologically integrated narrative methodology to enrich believers' stories for those who story with them—pastors, chaplains, community leaders, theological educators, and seminarians.

Stories are populated with people, and so I extend my thanks to many people.

I am thankful to the creators of stories that formed my training as a certified pastoral counselor, licensed marriage and family therapist, spiritual director, pastor, theological educator, and counseling center administrator. The first story was my theological education at Princeton Theological Seminary with thanks to the late Seward Hiltner who, until his retirement, was my doctoral advisor, a role then taken by James Lapsley and Don Capps. The second story is my narrative therapy training with thanks to Jill Freedman and Gene Combs at the Evanston Family Therapy Center and the teaching faculty of the Dulwich Centre in Adelaide, South Australia—Sekneh Beckett-Hammoud, David Denborough, Chris Dolman, David Epston, Jill Freedman, Stephen Madigan, Carolyn Markey, David Newman, and Cheryl White—where I received a Postgraduate Diploma in Narrative Therapy and Community Work.

Finally, a remembering of thanks goes to the late Michael White for inspiring me during his workshop on scaffolding conversations.

Thanks to the churches that shared stories of faith—Beech Fork Baptist Church, Hornerstown Baptist Church, First Baptist Community Church of Parsippany, Center City Baptist Chapel, Sparta Baptist Church, and New Freedom Baptist Church.

Thanks to the participants in my storytelling groups at Christian Theological Seminary, the Old National Road Presbyterian Parish, and First Baptist Church of Indianapolis.

Thanks to my students at Christian Theological Seminary.

Thanks to the administration and trustees of Christian Theological Seminary in extending a research leave.

Thanks to Ellen Corcella and Timothy Staveteig for copyediting.

Thanks to David Lott for introducing me to Fortress Press.

Thanks to Will Bergkamp, Lisa Gruenisen, and the publishing staff at Fortress Press.

Thanks to my husband Peter and son Joel for being the main characters in my story.

And, finally, thanks to my late parents and grandmother, Mama, Daddy, and Grandma whose voices and stories I carry with me.

1

Storying Spiritual Narratives

When is a story just a story? When is a story much more than a story? When is the story we think we know obscuring a much richer story? These questions and more lay at the root of my lifelong quest to understand the power of story. Growing up in a southern rural community, I learned the art of storytelling from my family and neighbors. I often heard with some admiration, "She sure is a good storyteller." I also heard with disapproval, "He sure can tell some big stories!"

I instinctively knew from both statements that some stories were cherished and brought forth life. Other stories were tall tales of deceit. My upbringing taught me that stories were a part of everyday life, stories influence your personal values, and stories influence how you value others. The "take away" for me was that stories tell us who a person is and is not. In my journey, I found it difficult to figure out how to identify and separate "good" stories from stories that were "tall tales."

My love for stories drew me to pastoral care because listening to others' stories carried such power. Those persons who had supportive stories in their lives seemed able to look to the future with at least a glimmer of hope. Those persons who focused on the stories of loss in their lives seemed to be unable to look, even for a second, at future possibilities.

Further complicating this caring for others through stories was my growing awareness that some stories were labeled as pathological while other stories were labeled as "normal." Never being one to value normality, I found this labeling more and more distressful. Pastoral diagnosing to an extreme seemed to negate the power of a living God who cares for us and struggles with us through pain to hope.

Listening for unique stories that tugged at me personally was part of who I was. However, I was quite surprised when I experienced a call to ministry in college. I was well aware that women were not expected to be ordained as

Southern Baptist ministers. Yet, my calling to the ministry was unmistakable. My home church, Beech Fork Baptist Church in Gravel Switch, Kentucky, ordained me after I graduated from seminary and began ministry. Soon, my world was shaken when the church was disfellowshipped from its association because I, a woman, was ordained there.

I had learned from my culture to work hard and trust God for one's calling. This learning seemed frail in the face of such opposition to women in ministry. Moving from an individually focused view—that I solely was responsible for my story—to a fuller view of how systems operate in stories and lives seemed to better explain both the oppression and the liberation. I sought an approach in my role as a pastoral counselor that expanded my individualistic approach to include an appreciation for family and organizational systems. This desire resulted in my studying family therapy at the Ackerman Institute for the Family.

Still, I yearned in my pastoral care and counseling practice to find an approach that would honor local stories, encourage the emergence of stories, and not hold a normative story as the standard for all stories. It was then I discovered narrative therapy. I first encountered narrative therapy through a workshop with Jill Freedman and Gene Combs. As I sat at the conference, I whispered to a colleague sitting by me, "This feels very theological." Since that experience, I stand by that story with the desire to develop narrative therapy through a theological perspective in liberation theology.

Through the years, I have sought to understand what makes narrative practice appealing to me. That connection comes, in part, from narrative therapy fiercely clinging to making meaning of people's lives. By making people authors of their life stories, narrative therapy finds value in common everyday experience, a discovery that, in turn, is valuable for people (M. White 2004).

Storying Narrative Understandings

I believe that narrative therapy offers a rich way to story and re-story our stories of everyday life as well as stories of faith. The power of using story in pastoral care and in ministry is evidenced by a trend in recent years seen through recent publications by the Alban Institute, wide-ranging topics in the Society of Pastoral Theology Annual Study Meeting, and other publications in pastoral care from a North American context.

Certainly, the word *narrative* cannot be copyrighted. It carries a wide range of meanings in pastoral care and ministry. My intent is to identify specific threads in the literature regarding the use of narrative therapy while also making the case for a narrower focus on narrative therapy and practice as co-developed by Michael White and David Epston.

Since the 1980s, a growing interest in narrative theory and practice has spread in ministry and theological studies as well as other disciplines. In addition to Michael White and David Epston, other postmodern thinkers such as Jerome Bruner, Howard Gardner, Clifford Geertz, Jacques Derrida, Paul Ricoeur, and Hans Frei have influenced the rise of narrative ministry models that, ultimately, influence people in the pew and their spirituality. Narrative theology, narrative preaching, and pastoral counseling in a narrative theme have each contributed to a narrative model for ministry that is now understood to address searching in a postmodern society where many of the master narratives of modern culture no longer exist (Golemon 2010a).

After reviewing the literature in pastoral care and ministry, I propose that current narrative approaches fall into three general categories: (1) broad narrative methodology, (2) genres of narratives or stories, and (3) psychotherapeutic narrative methodology. Let us discuss these narrative approaches and their contributions to pastoral care and ministry.

BROAD NARRATIVE METHODOLOGY

A *broad narrative methodology* focuses on how the telling of a life story and application of that story can aid in faith development and understandings of Christian belief. In this genre, Charles Scalise's *Bridging the Gap: Connecting What You Learned in Seminary with What You Find in the Congregation*, lifts up narrative theology and posits that it has the promise of healing the rift between history and theology. He argues that narrative provides a natural connection for linking an individual's story with the master stories of the Christian faith. Further, he believes that narrative offers a venue for including others in reflections on faith as individuals share their stories with others. While offering an accessible way to connect life with theology, he also notes that the narrative approach is too closely tied with human limitation and flaws (Scalise 2003).

Doehring's now-classic *The Practice of Pastoral Care: A Postmodern Approach* offers a specific approach to pastoral care that looks at the way careseekers share their lives with caregivers through the lens of premodern, modern, and postmodern perspectives. A *careseeker*, as defined by Doehring, is a person who desires pastoral care from a pastoral caregiver. Doehring argues that, at any one time, careseekers view their lives almost simultaneously from all three of those perspectives: literal and ritual premodern, critical modern, and postmodern relativist. Finally, in an appendix to her book, she explains her understanding of narrative pastoral care (Doehring 2006). One can argue that Doehring's work offers an overall postmodern sensibility and "narrative" feel.

A carefully constructed broad methodological approach to narrative comes from Golemon in the Narrative Leadership Collection. Drawing on narrative approaches informed by McAdams, Gardner, Bruner, and White through Foucault, he offers four principles of narrative leadership:

> 1. Redemptive stories of faith place human meaning within the scope of the divine in order to form persons, communities, and their normative values.
> 2. Narrative leaders in ministry use personal and symbolic intelligence to draw their congregations into story retrieval, construction, and response that is collaborative and intentional.
> 3. The choice of genre by redemptive motifs for a given story clarifies how the details of character and plot relate to a broader purpose for a faith community and what options of response are available to it.
> 4. Reconstructive narratives appeal to canonical understandings of tradition and practice but they invite the canon's deconstruction and renegotiation of a sign out of the tradition's vitality (Golemon 2010c).

In short, Golemon offers time, collaboration, genre, and canon as narrative principles of leadership for ministry. This leadership offers a rich variety of narrative approaches as interpreted by scholars, practitioners, and pastors.

Golemon further offers some intentions of narrative leadership in ministry:

> 1. Living and sharing God's story as leaders
> 2. Hearing people's stories and linking them to God's story
> 3. Creating a community of storytellers and actors
> 4. Reframing traditions and past for a healthy future
> 5. Engaging world stories with stories of faith
> 6. Discerning God's call to a new story in this place
> 7. Embodying congregations' new stories in renewed practices (Golemon 2010a)

Both Doehring and the Alban Institute's methodological approaches are sensitive to the changing world of pastoral care and ministry in its postmodern context while having a few distinctions. Doehring's approach integrates postmodern theories with modern psychotherapeutic approaches for a pastoral care model that can be used in a variety of cultural contexts. The most distinct characteristic of Doehring's work is that she intends it to be limited to pastoral care and not broadly applied to other ministry functions.

The principles and intentions of the Alban Institute's narrative leadership approach masterfully blend various sources using "narrative." In contrast to Doehring's work, this approach is specifically focused toward a broader pastoral ministry context and minimally concerned with pastoral care as a practice. At the same time, the strength of this approach is that it recognizes the richness of individuals and communities telling their own stories without outside interpretation. As individual and community stories are told and retold, the stories gain a vitality that enables the storytellers to envision these stories into the future. This approach, with its multiple practitioners, endeavors to connect life stories of faith and culture with the sacred story of God. The limitation is that the identified narrative approaches represent a rich variety of ministry settings that are idiosyncratic to their own cultural and faith contexts. In short, while the principles are quite descriptive, a specific practice orientation that can apply to various settings while honoring the local context is absent.

GENRES OF NARRATIVES OR STORIES

The second category of narrative approaches focuses on the genres of narratives or stories. In this approach, narratives or stories are categorized according to their type of story, then applications are made to pastoral ministry from these genres. Two helpful examples of this approach can be found in Edward Wimberly's *Recalling Our Own Stories* and Donald Capps's *Living Stories*. Wimberly identifies myths that he contends are harmful to the emotional and spiritual health of caregivers. These focus around personal myths, marital and family myths, and ministry myths. He references White and Epston's re-authoring as a way for caregivers to counter these myths with their own personal stories so that they may be renewed (Wimberly 1997).

The re-authoring found in Wimberly's book offers potential for re-authoring. However, the approach is not scrupulously true to narrative therapy practice. The myths here offer some structure for caregivers to identify what is sapping their strength. At the same time, a normative genre of myth exists that may be actually too simplistic when trying to understand how personal stories are oppressed by other stories. A critical question emerges about whether one can say that one's personal story is always healing. Does it not have limitations?

Capps loosely follows the same method by identifying three story genres that are life-giving rather than life-defeating. The inspirational story utilizes the power of suggestion, the paradoxical story works at "untying knots," and the miracle story identifies the exception from problems in people's stories. Capps helpfully uses a postmodern psychotherapeutic sensibility, making some reference to White and Epston but largely referring to solution-focused therapy, an approach pioneered by Steve de Shazer and Insoo Kim Berg. He offers helpful detail for ministers about how this theory actually works in the congregational setting (Capps 1998).

Both approaches have limitations in their focus on story from one context—the personal for Wimberly and the congregational for Capps. I believe people find categories and types of narrative largely helpful in providing some structure for their reflection, but trying to meet the normality inherent in genres can be ultimately oppressive and limiting.

Psychotherapeutic Narrative Methodology

The last narrative category to discuss is the psychotherapeutic narrative methodology. Outstanding examples of this approach are found with the works of Christie Neuger, Duane Bidwell, and Richard Hester and Kelli Walker-Jones. All three approaches are true to the technique and spirit of narrative therapy as co-developed by White and Epston. I find this discovery so refreshing after reading some literature that claims to be "narrative" in the approach of White and Epston but upon reading bears little resemblance to narrative therapy. Neuger explores the "dominant cultural discourse" of gender in her volume dedicated to narratively counseling women (2001). Bidwell offers an accessible approach for pastors to the spiritual care of couples that is true to narrative therapy. His book offers a rich source of questions that pastors can use in their work with couples (2013). The only limitation to the approaches advocated in the two books is the rather sophisticated level of pastoral care skills pastors should possess in order to implement their proposed narrative practices.

Rounding out the psychotherapeutic narrative approach is Hester and Walker-Jones's book on clergy peer groups, which was supported by a grant from the Lilly Foundation. The book offers rich insights from several years of work with a group of clergy as they struggle with both personal and pastoral identity. Such a group is well suited to narrative therapy with its powerful emphasis on the ways stories support meaning in our identities. Hester and Walker-Jones use re-authoring or re-storying in a group process to enable participants to acknowledge their stories and what emerges freely for them with those stories that they have carried from their faith communities (Hester and Walker-Jones 2009). The narrative informed approach is clearly presented so that it can be replicated in other settings.

The only major work of psychotherapeutic narrative methodology that does not fit so nicely in these categories is Andrew Lester's *Hope in Pastoral Care and Counseling*. True to the theory of White and Epston's narrative therapy, Lester offers a pastoral theology that infuses a theology of hope from Moltmann with the spirit of narrative therapy, offering pastoral theologians and pastoral ministers' insight to light their journeys of discovery. In many ways, it lifts up the best of all three categories.

FUTURE STORYING

How, then, does the narrative methodology of this book offer something distinct from the approaches discussed previously?

First, this inaugural methodology joins the narrative therapy of White and Epston to the cutting-edge collective narrative practice of Cheryl White and David Denborough of the Dulwich Centre in South Australia. I believe this book uses the collective narrative approach for the first time in North American pastoral care and ministry. These approaches connect the divide between individual and family therapy and community work based on the same theoretical framework. Using a common theoretical framework will strengthen the methodology so that comparisons and applications can be made more readily—beginning with a narrow focus of pastoral care, moving to a broader span of congregational ministry, and ending with community social justice.

Second, applying this narrative methodology to this spectrum of pastoral ministry gives the reader an opportunity to delve more richly into one approach. By concentrating on one approach, quite paradoxically, the pastoral practitioner has a clearer map to follow when deciding to travel on unmarked roads. Then, when returning to the main road, he or she can travel with more confidence while exuding an adventuresome spirit in looking for the next unmarked road.

Third, following in a relatively "pure" manner, White and Epston's narrative therapy puts this material closer to the anthropological origins of the approach gleaned from Gregory Bateson.[1] This methodology honors, in many

---

1. Narrative resources in this book represent the current thinking in narrative practice rather than relying primarily upon White and Epson's 1990 book. Epston expressed concern at such approach in my narrative training at the Dulwich Centre.

ways, the increasing bent of pastoral theology to practice a public theology that opens itself to multiple disciplines beyond the behavioral sciences. Further, its anthropological foundation recognizes cultural sensitivity and priority to local experiences.

Fourth, narrative therapy's emphasis on "privilege" and its oppressive effects on human lives will be acknowledged in this volume. Historically, Cheryl White brought a feminist consciousness to narrative therapy so that feminism is a foundation rather than an addition to narrative as acknowledged by Michael White (White 1995). In addition to sexism, other privileged voices of oppression such as racism, sexism, ageism, ableism, and heteronormativity exist in our lives. Our struggle is to identify what privilege we honor at any one time and recognize it as having the potential to rob people of their future hopes and dreams.

Fifth, the narrative emphasis on "practice" values the pastoral skills of ministry as equal to scholarly and academic endeavors. Connected with a praxis ethos, the narrative stance of the therapist as being "de-centered and influential" (White, 2005) can refocus attention on the value of being a pastor in the face of cultural norms valuing executives and specialized ministers. White uses this concept of *de-centered and influential* to emphasize the role of the therapist or caregiver as creating a non-hierarchial relationship that, nevertheless, endeavors to gently lift up generative possibilities that emerge in a person's life. At the same time, the careseeker is always understood to be the "expert" on their lives and not the therapist or caregiver. This means that the careseeker has knowledge about his or her life that the caregiver can never know.

The emphasis on issues of transference/countertransference touted in pastoral care and counseling can lead such care and counseling to concentrate on the "psychological" rather than embracing the "spiritual" of pastoral ministry. The de-centered stance of the narrative practitioner focuses on the humanity of the caregiver while honoring the expert status of the careseeker.

Thus, a pastoral ministry informed by narrative approaches will enable church members, hospital patients, or community persons to trust themselves more fully rather than seeing their human frailties as pathological. In addition, the narrative practitioner's "influential" rather than "expert" role acknowledges the caregiver's own pastoral skills, which encourages the careseeker to claim his or her own story. Blending both of these qualities will, I believe, move the emphasis of theological education from equipping the ministers to building mutually collaborative relationships between leaders and laity, walking together.

Sixth, this book includes two pieces of contextual experiences. The first is qualitative research based on collective narrative practice called the Staff of Spirit, which is a spiritual formation group process. The second contribution is a pedagogical methodology of a cultural immersion class taught in Appalachia that focuses on the re-storying of local stories into stories of faith.

Seventh, spiritual narratives are understood in a new way that binds stories, storytelling, and storyteller. Stories belong to the storyteller who has lived the story. The story can be told to oneself and to God. It can be richly thickened as it is told to others whose very listening shapes the story itself. Stories can be written, shared orally, or both written and shared orally. The telling of the story itself to the listeners can result in a thickening of the story in the storyteller's experience (Narativ, Inc. 2013).

Eighth, the weaving of liberation theology, narrative therapy, collective narrative practice, and real life experience comprises a unique approach to pastoral care and ministry. Experiences of laity are honored while at the same time ministers in various ministries are encouraged to lift up their unique contributions to laity. At this beginning juncture, I name this approach liberative narrative ministry.[2]

Before moving on the bridge toward spiritual narrative, it is important to introduce the North American theological community to collective narrative practice, which will be more fully developed in future chapters. Collective narrative practice intends to take away the delineation between what is individual and what is community. The methodology, based on the following principles, was developed in responding to trauma people face around the globe:

1. To listen for double-storied accounts—descriptions not only of trauma but of the ways the person responded to trauma
2. To find a way to richly acknowledge the real effects of the abuse the person experienced
3. To link the person's life and experiences to some sort of collective
4. To enable the person to make a contribution to the lives of others
5. To conceive of the person as representing a social issue
6. To enable the person to join a collective endeavor in addressing, in some local way, that social issue
7. To enable people to speak through us, not just to us (Denborough 2008)

2. "Liberative" comes from Loren Townsend's *Introduction to Pastoral Counseling;* narrative therapy as developed by Michael White and David Epston; and collective narrative practice as developed by David Denborough and Cheryl White.

BRIDGES TO SPIRITUAL NARRATIVES

These collective narrative principles focus broadly on listening to multiple levels of a story and finding ways that the person telling the story can thicken it through broadening life experiences. Also, importantly, the storyteller uses the social issue represented in the story to connect with others struggling with the same oppression. Collective narrative practice is a way of expanding individual experience to include others.

Blending the distinctions of a narrowly focused narrative methodology accomplishes a few tasks that enrich pastoral care and ministry and their effects on congregants and community members. It invites multiple voices to be present when collaborating. It lessens the oppression of the so-called normative "right" way to do things in church. It understands that adding complexity rather than oversimplifying a problem is more generative. It understands that interdisciplinary collaboration is more nurturing than the current divisions present in ministry and theological education.

I argue now that Seward Hiltner, many years ago, offered a foundation to pastoral theology that would honor these premises. In his pioneering work, *Preface to Pastoral Theology*, written in the 1950s, Hiltner offers what was then and truly is now a startling premise: pastoral ministry is interlaced with multiple viewpoints that are always present and always influencing each other. He calls this approach the perspectival approach—truly simple yet brilliant (Hiltner 1958). Hiltner's perspectival approach helpfully addressed the dilemma of theological specialization that promoted and still promotes the insular seminary education of future ministers. Also, inherent in the perspectival approach was theological reflection on pastoral activities. So, oddly, the argument Hiltner largely began—contending that pastoral theology was not applied theology but theology of a different approach—is still being discussed.

Theological reflection on pastoral activities undergirded Hiltner's concern for the fledgling field of pastoral counseling. In my work with Hiltner as a masters and doctoral student, he always emphasized the need for pastoral counseling not to become over "psychologized" and separate from the life of the church. Thus, theological reflection must always utilize contributions from psychotherapy in an integrative enterprise.

Hiltner's perspectival approach lends itself as a foundation to the multiple voicing that narrative practice calls for. Moreover, it expands narrative's foundation of anthropology and its emphasis on acknowledging personal biases that is so critical in our global world. These emphases enrich a search for stories of faith that church members, community members, and congregations hold. Then, the uncovering of spiritual narratives can occur as believers find unclaimed stories that deepen their faith and ultimately strengthen them while living in a culture where narratives of meaning are largely absent. The uncovering of spiritual narratives is enabled by revisiting the meaning of spirituality with its goal of thickening spiritualties in people's lives. Now we move to understanding more deeply the power of story and the way in which spirituality emerges from it.

STORYING SPIRITUALITY

Much of these pastoral ministries' interest in narrative studies originates from the rich use of stories in the Bible. Biblical stories illustrate how people can live and the possibilities of life in a faith context (Metayard 2008). Biblical stories are more than just "stories" in an everyday sense. They serve to connect believers to a God who offers possibilities for people beyond their everyday vision. Stanley Hauerwas says, "We are a 'storied people' because the God that sustains us is a 'storied God'" (Hauerwas 1981, 91).

In my earlier book, *Re-storying Your Faith*, I present several ideas that are developed in this book. This "storied identity" is built through multiple layers of experiences that go beyond the chronological order of events. As people interpret events in their lives, they develop a sense of who they are quite apart from the actual historicity of events. This "interpretative scheme," according to George Stroup, includes ideals, values, preferences, and goals. In turn, Christian identity is formed from the interpretation of these stories into "identity narratives" that stand up against Christian narratives (Meteyard 2008, 100).

The form in which people choose to interpret their stories into these narratives is critical and has a direct effect on how people live out those narratives. For example, if a person reframes a story of having to overcome obstacles in a context of tragedy rather than liberation, it takes on a very different form. Finally, a part of people's narratives important in religious life is the ability to disrupt and reform canons of meaning inherited from religious tradition.

In a Christian context, biblical writers often take an accepted metaphor or symbol and then change the meaning of that metaphor to make the narrative more meaningful. An example of changing the canon of meaning can be seen in Paul's use of the old Adam and the new Adam as he explains the power of transformation in life when one is transformed in the image of Christ rather than the human image of Adam (Golemon 2010c).

The lifting up of common, everyday experiences to create a full meaning of life uses a very human vehicle—story—to accomplish its task. Through story, we as humans create a cohesive understanding of what has happened to us—both good and bad. As we move through life, our past stories come along on the journey as we create new stories and anticipate new stories in the untraveled future.

Stories for people of faith through the centuries are about meaning. Through storytelling, believers have shared their spiritual experiences with others in the community of faith to strengthen their faith as well as the faith of fellow believers. Important beliefs of faith are conveyed through these stories both explicitly and implicitly. Spiritual stories are never neutral. They carry with them discourses of meaning. Often in the community of faith, certain stories are privileged. They are viewed as adhering to a "normal" route for faith development. Particular denominations may validate certain spiritual stories that support their doctrinal beliefs.

What happens then when believers, through the vicissitudes of life, have stories that challenge those privileged stories of faith? This question piques my interest and provides direction for this book in developing narrative practice as an approach to uncover spiritual narratives. To that end, let us create a working definition of spirituality.

Naming Spirituality

Spirituality is defined in many ways. Spirituality may refer to a rather expansive sense of being uplifted. Others define spirituality as some kind of practice, such as working with the homeless, which gives their lives meaning beyond themselves. For other people, spirituality can name anything that gives life meaning quite separate from belief in any deity. Ecological concerns, social service, meditation, psychotherapy all have aspects of spirituality that move their practitioners beyond themselves.

Exploring spiritual narratives requires a Christian definition of spirituality that specifically draws on the sacred story of Christian faith and the faith stories of believers. Further, distinctions and commonalities between spirituality and religion will create a methodology for exploring spiritual narratives in multiple faith contexts.

Spirituality and religion are understood to overlap while having different constructs. In a Christian context, spirituality is understood as a relationship with God that gives a sense of meaning in life. Religion is understood as the formalized structuring of spirituality so that it may be transmitted from person to person and generation to generation. It is formed in community with people who have had similar experiences (Hodge 2005). As soon as even a few people share a similar spiritual experience, religion starts to form. In the beginning of a religion, the experience of believers forms a personal spiritual connection. All believers of a new religion hope that such spiritual connection would continue. This hope, however, is not always realized. When religion loses its spiritual connection, new stories of spirituality need to be uncovered with the support of a rich definition of spirituality.

Spirituality in a Christian context is thus defined here as "that meaning from life that encompasses an experience bigger than self and relationships sparked by connecting with God through Jesus Christ as co-creator of story and the Spirit as sustainer of story" (Coyle 2011b). With this focus, spirituality draws from people's lives the very deepest experiences from which meanings emerge, forming foundational beliefs that people that can return to again and again. This spirituality links believers to Jesus Christ through both personal and community experiences and motivates them to look for meaning in those transformative experiences that connect them closer to Christ. As these experiences form into stories, hearers or readers then experience profound transformation through Jesus who engages believers in discovering and expanding their faith stories. From here, we will look at how spirituality is being expanded through narrative practices in the church and ministry studies and how the narrative practice in this book is both similar and different from those studies.

Storying Spiritual Narratives

Common and sacred stories are then an essential thread of believers' faith, their congregations' identities, and their communities' futures. Only by telling those stories, others re-telling those stories, and the community members re-telling the re-telling of the stories can a tapestry of faith stories emerge (Coyle 2010). This tapestry shows the rough nubs of pain as well as the beauty of life's colors. Its multiple layers of thread give it strength to better withstand the wear and tear of life.

Spiritual narratives are at the same time both faith stories and not faith stories. One can share a story about his or her faith journey, which I later refer to as "formative spiritual experience" (Coyle 2013). I can tell a story about an encounter with God. If that story remains isolated, it is just a story. It may have meaning at some times, and at other times it seems rather ethereal. If I take that story and reflect deeply about it, I may discover that that story reminds me of another story in some kind of "aha" moment. The more I reflect on that initial story and the other stories connected with it, the stronger those stories become. Then, I share those stories with my best friend. She responds to those stories. Surprisingly, I have a different perspective of those stories. Together with my remembrances and my friend's re-telling, I now am beginning to experience a similar and different story than the first initial story.

Further, the initial story and the subsequent storying bring to my mind some stories that are not explicitly spiritual. I think further about those stories. Then, suddenly, as if from nowhere, I think about the seemingly "nonspiritual" stories. I may reflect with fondness on a family trip when I was a child. Such "nonspiritual" stories seem to fit with the "spiritual" stories with a new richness.

This journey of imagination lifts up the essential qualities of spiritual narratives. Spiritual narratives are those stories that are bound together with meaning and serve as a source of strength that one can draw on in the face of hardship. Spiritual narratives weave multiple stories that span the past, present, and future of our lives. They can be explicitly spiritual or have an implicit spirituality.

I have named these spiritual narratives "spiritual" because I believe that we too often compartmentalize our lives so that even when we have a spiritual moment, some of us are likely to explain it away. On the other end of the spectrum, some of us believers may be apt to think of everything as explicitly spiritual. My notion of a spiritual narrative is a resilient story that connects with both the sacred and common of life in a way that lifts us out of ourselves and our relationships to yearn to view the world and its people through God's eyes.

Further, spiritual narratives are never static. Unlike the initial conversion experience we tell over and over again without change, spiritual narratives are told over and over again and become richer with each re-telling. They are flexible yet strong, engaging yet distinctive. Change does not threaten a spiritual narrative. New life experiences do not weaken a spiritual narrative because those stories are woven in with the old and new.

Spiritual narratives do not listen to normative stories for what they should be. They listen to lost stories that may offer rich guides for hopes and dreams of the future. Spiritual narratives are not fixed in the past, hoping that all pain and disappointment will be worked through. Spiritual narratives live in the present, honor the past as teacher, and look forward to the promise of the future.

Spiritual narratives do not see only theological language and religious places as being friend. They see the world God created as embracing both the common and the sacred under God's care. At the same time, spiritual narratives do not think that spiritual language is unnecessary. At times, what is spiritual can only be expressed in spiritual language. The words themselves "enflesh" God's presence in the believer's spiritual experience. Words become more than just words. Spiritual words express the immanent dwelling of the Spirit in the life of each believer. The Logos in John says, "In the beginning was the word and the word was God" (John 1:1, NRSV). Words are more than representations. They embody who the person is (Coyle 2007).

Stories of faith, in a similar way, enflesh the believer's spiritual identity. They are more than events and places. They sometimes aspire to be symbolic as well as true experiences that enrich one's faith. A believer makes meaning out of stories, and the story, in turn, becomes past, present, and future experiences. Narrative practice as developed in the next chapter will offer an approach that honors storytelling in a deeper way.

PRACTICES

- Think of a simple story that occurred to you within the last day. It needs to not be excessively complicated, painful, or sad. Then, turn to the person sitting beside you. As the storyteller, take five minutes to tell the story to your partner. The partner is to listen attentively. Then, in the next two minutes, the partner is to tell the story back to you. Conclude by sharing with the listener what connected with you as authentic in the listening and retelling of the story. The listener now becomes the storyteller in the same procedure. Conclude by discussing for five minutes what make the telling of the story and the listening of the story difficult or simple. Attend to the process, not the content.
- Share with another person what you know about how you got your name. Who selected the name? Were you named for someone? What is the effect of that knowledge on you and who you are? Take turns. (Adapted from an exercise at Dulwich Centre in Adelaide, South Australia.)

2

Voicing Narrative and Liberation Practices

Spiritual narratives, as identified in the previous chapter, draw from both an explicit and implicit theological grounding as well as from insights of narrative practice. Providing a multivoiced conversation between narrative therapy and liberation theology is essential in laying both theological and practice focused foundations for uncovering those spiritual narratives. Narrative therapy provides a psychotherapeutic approach supportive of life stories. Liberation theology supports a spirituality focused on social justice. Both common life and transcendent spiritual experiences populate spiritual narratives in people's lives. We now embark on a discussion about narrative therapy, liberation theology, and the paths of discovery between them.

BEGINNING TO STORY NARRATIVE THERAPY

Narrative therapy emerged from the postmodern rumblings of the 1980s in which major fields of inquiry began to examine modern assumptions about life. Focal understandings included the assertion that metanarratives of understanding our world were no longer viable. This assertion continues to this day and evokes, at times, heated discussions between those who maintain that absolute values and metanarratives still exist and those who maintain that metanarratives do not exist.

Large metanarratives espousing values and providing stability, I maintain, do not largely exist in our culture. At the same time, important values of belief in God still inform our lives. These beliefs vary from person to person. Believers struggle to find some linkage to Scripture, Christian tradition, and the contemporary church that connects to their everyday experiences. The challenge for today's Christians is to affirm spiritual beliefs and relationship to God in a way that allows for growth with changes in everyday life.

Narrative therapy offers a postmodern perspective of the world that I believe is compatible with liberation theology. Here, I discuss the theoretical foundations of narrative therapy, explicate some of narrative therapy's practices, and then connect these with pastoral practices. Narrative therapy has a foot in two worlds—the postmodern reflection of Michel Foucault and the narrative metaphor of Jerome Bruner. Understanding a specific definition of *narrative* is most important. I then explore specific narrative therapy practices that can be used in pastoral care and ministry. Finally, I lift up some narrative principles that have links to liberation theology.

A two-storied understanding of narrative lays a foundation for narrative therapy (Payne 2006). One understanding of narrative therapy focuses on a common definition of narrative, defined as a series of events that constitute a story. Story can be used interchangeably with narrative in this sense. As people tell their personal stories, they identify who they are in terms of their history, their present life, and their various life roles and relationships. Additionally, a story has future movement in either anticipating an outcome or wishing for an alternate outcome to the story (Payne 2006). Thus, stories do not need to have a definitive interpretation to be a story. One's experience of the story is primary; eventually the storyteller gives meaning to the story, which is quite different from interpreting the story.

The common use of story or narrative in ministry studies certainly focuses on this understanding. Additionally, some counseling claiming to be narrative therapy follows this understanding rather than an understanding truer to White and Epston's conception. The blending of a postmodern understanding of narrative is what sets apart the narrative therapy understanding used in this book. We now turn to this level of understanding.

This understanding focuses on the postmodern concept of narrative championed by Paul Ricoeur. In *Time and Narrative* (1984), he contends that narrative is the mental structuring process through which we define our existential relationship with the physical and conceptual worlds. This expanded postmodern understanding of narrative, along with other postmodern thinking, focuses on the legitimacy of multiple descriptions of life and the world. Many therapies use story as a means to understand a person's problems. Approaches to narrative such as Riceour's typically understand a normative story to exist that will be more helpful for resolving the client's problems. A postmodern therapeutic understanding of narrative, however, values the multiplicity of many stories that are to be identified by the client.

Further, more objective and scientifically friendly perspectives exist in psychotherapy. A narrative therapy that is informed by postmodernism understands our everyday stories to be only a part of the complexity of our lives as we live them. The stories that we tell ourselves and others are not only representations of memory but are also influential in our lives. These stories form the beliefs by which we understand our lives and our world. Further, an interaction exists between "the stories we tell ourselves about our lives, the ways we live our lives, and the further stories we then tell" (Payne 2006, 26).

Michael White provides a clear definition of story or narrative in an interview:

> This is to propose that human being are interpreting beings—that we are active in the interpretation of our experiences as we live our lives. It's to propose that it's not possible for us to interpret our experience without access to some frame of intelligibility, one that provides a context for our experience, one that makes the attribution of meaning possible. It's to propose that stories constitute this frame of intelligibility. It's to propose that the meanings derived in this process of interpretation are not neutral in their effects on our lives, but have real effects on what we do, on the steps that we take in life. It's to propose that it is the story or self-narrative that determines which aspects of our lived experience get expressed, and it is to propose that it is the story [or] self-narrative that determines the shape of lived experience. It's to propose that we live by the stories that we have about our lives, that these stories actually shape our lives, constitute our lives and that they "embrace" our lives (1995, 13–14).

Using narrative or story in a postmodern vein is different from a more traditional use of narrative commonly employed in our culture and some ministry studies. "Interpreting" narratives in postmodern thinking refers to the way in which people make sense of or "interpret" their own stories through their own lenses. This approach is in distinct contrast to other psychotherapeutic theories in which a therapist may offer a person an interpretation of the person's life experience which is then placed in a normative context (Payne 2006).

In narrative therapy, the therapist understands the "interpreting" or making meaning function to belong to the person to whom the story belongs. The "storytelling rights" of the story, hence, belong to the owner or author of the story and not to the professional (Madigan 2011). Further, stories from narrative therapy do not place a psychological lens on the interpretation of the story. Rather, it is assumed that people make sense of their stories through cultural or social lenses rather than through psychology (Payne 2006).

Thus, in narrative therapy it becomes important to determine the avenue by which a person shares his or her story. That avenue is language, and, by extension, postmodern therapies emphasize strongly the importance of language. Both verbal and written language has the potential to clarify meaning, to distort meaning, or to oversimplify. Through language, we tell the stories to a public audience that we may often tell over and over again to ourselves.

Yet, stories carry with them not only our personal wording and rewording of life experience but also the wording of the cultures in which we live. People can easily come to believe that their personal experiences should conform to normative meanings. The result can be a pinched sense of identity as people struggle to make themselves fit in the norms that culture can often impose upon us all.

The purpose of narrative therapy becomes to listen to language as critically influencing the way in which people see themselves, their experiences, and their relationships. People can experience a loss of identity when their experience of who they really are does not conform to the normative cultural view (Payne 2006). Narrative therapy refers to this cultural "metanarrative" as a "dominant cultural discourse"—something that permeates the very air in which we live. These dominant cultural discourses carry with them an idea of what is "normal" with regard to gender, sexual orientation, race, socioeconomic status, disability, work achievement, age, and so on.

Narrative therapy as understood in this book consciously takes on a postmodern view of challenging these dominant cultural discourses. While many of the metanarratives that humanity once understood as permeating and ruling our everyday lives no longer exist, postmodernism is not the dominant mode of thinking in the world. Modernism as a philosophical way of thinking is still predominant.

Postmodern thinking at its very core emphasizes the deconstruction of belief to analyze what is there—in short, to ask why (Payne 2006). Michael White once said that psychotherapy had taken away a perfectly good word—"why" (2007). Postmodern thinking examines all assumptions and beliefs, understanding that what we identify as "us" and "our own" is contained in the stories we tell others and ourselves.

Postmodernism maintains skepticism toward science and does not believe that all science is purely objective. This thinking about science is currently in the conversation among scientists who discuss observer effect. Postmodernism assumes that all knowledge is provisional, socially and politically influenced, and linked with social power (Payne 2006). So, science is redefined not as a superior way of knowing but another peculiar way of knowing.

Another common viewpoint about postmodernism is that it abhors all values and is morally vacuous. In strong contrast, Michael White strongly advocated for the necessary ethical dimension of the role of the therapist. In one article, he contended that the therapist must carefully attend to the therapist's influence on the client and forwarded a "de-centered but influential" role in which the ethics of the client reign supreme and the therapist respects the person while at the same time trying to influence good in that person's life (M. White 2000a).

The postmodernism utilized by narrative therapy loudly asks the question, "why"? Then, the deconstruction of beliefs begins with reexamining all beliefs and modern ideas, looking first at one side, then at the other, and finally restructuring those beliefs in a new way. The process is ongoing, and values and beliefs are considered to be essential but always fodder for fresh viewpoints.

The person and the person's beliefs become the critical locus for exploring ways of knowing from a narrative practitioner's perspective. These ways of knowing understand local knowledge to be as important as expert knowledge. At the same time, they do not elevate local knowledge to a superior position over modern or scientific knowledge.

The critical link between local knowledge and narrative therapy comes through the form in which local knowledge is expressed. Whether engaging in a conversation, writing a biography, or discussing a problem in therapy, a person expresses his or her local knowledge in the form of a story (Payne 2006). In fact, these stories we tell ourselves about ourselves form our sense of who we are: "For the last several years, I have been looking at another kind of thought, one that is quite different in form from reasoning: the form of thought that goes into the constructing not of logical or inductive arguments but of stories or narratives. . . . [J]ust as it is worthwhile examining in minute detail how physics or history go about their world making, might we not be well advised to explore in equal detail what we do when we construct ourselves autobiographically?" (Bruner 1987a, 120).

Our experiential knowledge blends our personal meanings into how we understand ourselves from a first-person perspective. In contrast, expert knowledge asserts that it is objective. Yet, narrative therapy would question whether a therapist who offers "expert" knowledge can ever be objective. The experiential knowledge of narrative therapy comes from the understanding of local knowledge as defined by Geertz (1983). This type of knowledge refers to both individual and community knowledge. Community knowledge is that which may be passed on culturally from one generation to another. Often, that kind of understanding flies in the face of modern improvements in community. Such an example might be the objectives of a person who lives in a run-down house in a supportive community who is being moved to a new, fully staffed nursing home far away from her home community. This woman's local knowledge recognizes that a modern facility would not offer the same support as her native community, something that might not be evident to "logical" understandings of the situation.

Narrative therapy takes this understanding of knowledge from Geertz and further situates it in Geertz's metaphors of "thin" and "thick" to describe life experience (1973). White borrows these metaphors and uses the term *thin* to describe a person's culturally influenced unexamined beliefs and the term *thick* to refer to richly complex understanding of one's life experience and beliefs. Inherent is this deconstructing process is the understanding that culturally formed bases of power often mitigate against people examining their lives and beliefs. In this way, reexamined beliefs can be fully enriching.

Moving into this understanding of thick and thin descriptions of one's life will be readily discussed as it applies to the traditional notion self. "Self," as largely understood in psychotherapy as well as theology, espouses a notion of a core self. While some psychotherapies may discuss a real self, an ideal self, and so on, the basic understanding is that each person has a core self that is really the self to which one must be true. The narrative premise is that each person has multiple selves being influenced by multiple relationships and locations. Thus, for a narrative therapist, it is desirable for persons to examine and reexamine their multiple selves to determine which relational selves offer thicker descriptions of life experiences that can enhance their future hopes and dreams.

The development of relational or multiple selves is based on an individual having the power to examine and reexamine longheld identities and beliefs. These identities and beliefs are understood through Foucault's analysis of power and knowledge. Foucault contended that subordinate persons are kept in a subordinate position by persons in positions of power. Power is obtained by acquiring expert knowledge and keeping that knowledge to oneself. As subordinates gain different types of knowledge, the person in authority or institution in power maintains the idea that a desirable normative belief exists.

The subordinate is then told that the knowledge he or she possesses is not adequate.

Thus, for Michael White, the problem stories that people bring to therapy are often attached to unexamined cultural discourses that oppress a person's agency in claiming his or her own self-knowledge. The goal for narrative therapy then becomes empowering people to reexamine their problem saturated stories so that they are able to eventually re-author or re-story[1] their life stories and, through telling and retelling stories and subplots, develop a richer life story. To understand this telling and retelling process, several narrative practices will be described.

NARRATIVE PRACTICES

Among the narrative practices used in the telling and retelling process are the following: externalizing, re-authoring or re-storying, ceremonial definitions, re-membering, scaffolding, and the absent but implicit. Other practices exist, but I believe that having a working familiarity with these practices will enable the theologian or minister to practice narratively in a ministry setting.

EXTERNALIZING

Externalizing conversations serve as antidote to people understanding their identity as intertwined with their problem. In its basic form, externalizing objectifies the problem "against cultural objectification of people. This makes it possible for people to experience an identity that is separate from the problem; the problem becomes the problem, not the person" (M. White 2007).

As people externalize their problems, a liminal space is created whereby they are able to stand outside the problems. In this space, then, it becomes possible to reflect on their relationship to the problems themselves. What is their impact upon their lives? Who in their lives do the problems affect? When do they notice the problems? How do they see themselves when the problems are present?

These kinds of externalizing questions can be helpfully facilitated through a *statement of position map*, which Michael White postulated shortly before his death. Such maps are possible routes to get someplace with people and their

---

1. Re-authoring, re-storying, and re-membering, as used in narrative therapy, are spelled with a hyphen.

problems. However, it is not necessary to limit one's care of another to these maps.

The purpose of a *statement of position map* is to provide a context whereby adults and even young children can be consulted about what is important in their lives. By engaging in this kind of consultation, people often feel more confident about their own ability to make decisions about their lives in the face of their problems. As people gain personal agency, the therapist is able to demonstrate that he or she does not provide the answers for clients' lives while at the same time introducing the context that will enable clients to gain strength in the face of their problems (M. White 2007).

The statement of position map has four categories of inquiry. The first is "negotiating a particular experience-near definition of the problem" (M. White 2007, 40). An "experience-near" definition of the problem stresses the importance of people naming their problems in a way that makes sense for them. It is based on their personal understanding of life.

The second stage in developing externalizing conversations inquires about the effects or influence of the problem in the areas of the person's life. Common areas include home, workplace, school, and peers; relationships with others and relationship with oneself; identity and effect of the problem on one's hopes, dreams, and values; and one's future possibilities.

The third stage is evaluating the effects of the problem's activities. Questions of inquiry include the following: "Are these activities okay with you? How do you feel about these developments? What is your position on what is unfolding here? Is this development positive or negative—or both, or neither, or something in between?" (M. White 2007, 44).

The last category of inquiry is "justifying the evaluation." It proudly explores the "why" of people's lives with questions largely vilified by psychotherapy. Some questions include the following: "Why is/isn't this okay for you? Why do you feel this way about this development?" The questions here are not moral judgments. The intention is to help people give voice to their understandings of their lives and develop understandings of their intentions in life (M. White 2007). These categories of inquiry do not always follow a linear progression, nor should they. Further, not all narrative conversations must begin with externalizing. It is a tool to be used if and when it is needed.

RE-AUTHORING OR RE-STORYING

Re-authoring or re-storying is a critical narrative practice. In this description, I will use the term *re-authoring* since it is the most common term in narrative therapy. However, as the use of story is developed in this book, I will use the term *re-storying* since I contend it has more fluency in pastoral ministry. As people describe problems and dilemmas in their lives, they unfold in the form of stories that link the events of their lives in a theme over time. In re-authoring, people are invited to develop and tell stories about their lives and are helped to include the experiences that are "out of phase" with their dominant storylines. These events and experiences are called "unique outcomes" (M. White 2007, 81). These unique outcomes provide a starting point for re-storying conversations.

The role of the therapist is to encourage people to draw from their life experience as well as to evoke their imagination in visioning where activating unexplored areas of their experience could actually enliven their lives and relationships. As one maps a re-authoring conversation, two horizontal timelines—a landscape of action and a landscape of identity—serve to guide the person's taking authorship of his or her life story. The landscape of identity explores the storylines in terms of intentional understandings, what is accorded value, internal understandings and realizations, and learning and knowledge. The landscape of action includes event, circumstances, sequence, time, and plot.

Landscape of identity questions encourage the person to reflect on what he or she thinks about the event, what he or she feels about the event, what he or she has learned, what connection he or she sees in these events to the future. Further, identity questions focus around where the person's goals, aspirations, and hopes come from as well as how those formulations of identity are focused on beliefs, principles, and faith. Critically, the subjunctive nature of questions—using such words; *as, if, perhaps, possibly*—open the "interpretive process," according to White.

Again, this interpretive process opens new possible stories within the life of the person that are authored by the person and not the therapist. Finally, with great significance for theological inquiry, White posits, "Of all the responses that are invoked by landscape of identity questions, it is the intentional understandings and understanding that are centered on considerations of value that are the most significant with regard to rich story development" (1997, 100). Of course, the weaving of the landscape of events with the landscape of identity thickens story so that the individual has resilience. The landscape of events will remain barren if the landscape of identity with its meaning-making function is omitted.

RE-MEMBERING

Re-membering conversations are founded on the idea that identity is formed through relationships with others rather than through a core self. In re-membering conversations, people have the choice of deciding whose voices will be influential in their lives. People living and dead, pets, toys, books—all are candidates for these associations of life (M. White 2007). Deciding who or what to include in this association is an intentional process. Even history or biological connections do not have the ultimate say about what voices are important in one's life. The persons deciding have that authority.

Some questions for re-membering conversations include the following: Do you have any understanding about why this person is important in your life? What is your guess about how she or he contributed to your life? Do you know what that person valued in you? Do you have any idea about how his or her sense of her own life might have been different because of you? (M. White 2007).

A further use of re-membering comes in processing the grief experience when loved ones are lost. White's article "Saying Hullo Again: The Incorporation of the Lost Relationship in the Resolution of Grief" is a significant departure from the trend at that time of "working through" grief in the case of delayed grief reaction (1988). White understood that people had lost an important part of their own identity and postulated that they need to determine ways in which that person's voice can be heard again in their lives. Incorporating the lost relationship in the person's current life can be enriching. Some questions include the following: What contribution did that person make to your life? How might you incorporate those contributions to your current life? Lorraine Hedtke, an American narrative therapist, works extensively with applying narrative in working with grieving people.

DEFINITIONAL CEREMONIES

Definitional ceremonies in narrative therapy give people an opportunity to enrich their lives through the telling and retelling of stories before an audience of outsider witnesses. A typical social occasion where people tell the story of their lives or accomplishments evokes accolades or, if the stories are counter to cultural discourses, disapproval. Professional evaluation and applause are not a part of these definitional ceremonies (M. White 2007).

These ceremonies include conversation about the expressions in the telling of the story that caught their attention, the images that these expressions evoke, their own personal experience that resonated with those expressions, and a sense of how their lives have been touched by the expressions. Excessive praise, advice, or moralizing stories are not a part of the outsider witnesses' responses. The expressions of stories take many forms through this process of telling, retelling of the telling, and retelling of the retelling. The thickened stories are shared by the teller as well as the witnesses.

SCAFFOLDING

Scaffolding conversations were developed by White shortly before his death in 2008, using the work of Lev Vygotsky, a Russian educational psychologist. In scaffolding, the person recruits support from persons and extends life stories to move from what is known and familiar to what is not known and unfamiliar.

The purpose of scaffolding is to aid in three areas that are essential to personal development—personal agency, responsible action, and concept development. Personal agency connects in narrative therapy to the re-storying of life stories as persons develop the landscape of identity by initiating a process of making meaning of life events. Through meaning development, the person's agency is strengthened by actions that can then lead to deeper understandings of values and beliefs. As the person crosses this space, plans are made about finding adequate support as the transition from the known to the unknown is made. Learning from the experiences also becomes another step in influencing how the person would like her life story.

ABSENT BUT IMPLICIT

The *absent but implicit* carries great potential in lending support to how people restory their lives: "The notion of the 'absent but implicit' is informed by the understanding that all expression, and the meaning that expression conveys, is not derived directly from the experience of the 'thin' that expression refers to. . . . People's expressions of life do not apprehend the world out there as it is, whatever that world might be . . . that which is on the other side of what is being discerned, and upon what this discernment depends—that I am here referring to as the 'absent but implicit'" (M. White 2000, 37).

In focusing on the absent but implicit, a narrative therapist becomes concerned not only with the meanings people attribute to their life stories, but also how people came to understand their life stories. The absent but implicit brings questions that focus on hopes that things would be different in one's life, anticipation of arriving at a particular destination in life, dreams of a life lived more fully, and vision of new possibilities. By engaging with the absent but implicit, the therapist doubly listens through exploring the unstated. Thus, these types of therapeutic conversations are "double- or multi-storied conversations" (M. White 2000, 41).

MULTIVOICING NARRATIVE AND LIBERATION PRACTICES

Narrative therapy participates with liberation theology in a quest for social justice. Foundational to both perspectives is the recognition of the political reality of power and how power often oppresses people. Narrative practice's unique place among other therapeutic approaches is based on the staunch belief that the "problem" exists in dominant cultural discourses and not in the person. This is not to say that people have no agency or choice in their actions. Responsibility is important in narrative practice because its very intention is to thicken life stories to serve as resources for activism in one's life as well as one's families and communities.

Initial foci of liberation theology historically emphasized the importance of socioeconomic and political justice as evidenced through black and Latin American theologies. Increasing expansion of liberation theology to include theologies of oppressed groups such as women of all colors, gay persons, and persons with various disabilities has broadened its focus I contend to a theme that corresponds well with narrative— namely, that of privilege.

Liberating theologies believe that privilege occurs in everyday life in the communities of persons impacted by marginalization as well as the communities of persons not marginalized. A similar notion from narrative practice of privilege is to "describe unearned rights, benefits, immunity, and favours that are bestowed on individual and groups solely on the basis of their race, culture, religion, gender, sexual orientation, physical ability or key characteristics" (Raheim et al. 2009, 3).

Both narrative practice and liberation theology understand that both the oppressed and the oppressor participate in larger structures that take on a life of their own. Narrative practice refers to dominant cultural discourses in its understanding that language itself and stories actually embody the oppression of power brokers. Its premise is that through re-storying life stories through audiences of supportive communities, people will be able to gain sufficient strength to access multiple stories that eventually thicken their life stories.

I contend, however, that the transcendent dimension of life present in narrative practice could benefit from a thickened story through adding multiple voices of liberation theology. White discusses the ascendant, referring to the divine or God; the immanent, referring to the human spirit; and the immanent/

ascendant, which connects with divine in the self and a relationship with God. Despite acknowledgment of these spiritual dimensions, White's interest in the spiritual—which is passed on in "mainstream" narrative therapy—is a material version of spirituality based on visible aspects of people's lives that can be identified and developed, not on the "invisible" (White, Hoyt, and Combs 2000).

Three aspects of liberation theology—power, hope, and the Spirit—can add a chorus of voices to narrative practice. Liberation theology has been criticized as perhaps focusing too much on socioeconomic "this world" realities. However, power, hope, and the Spirit—essential aspects of liberative spirituality—have the capacity to thicken narrative's understanding of spirituality and its contribution of the transcendent or ascendant. In turn, liberation theology can thicken its own voice by inviting the transcendent into the everyday lives of person who face marginalization.

In highlighting these components of liberative spirituality, I will focus primarily on the method of liberation theology rather than its sheer content.[2] The methods of both liberation theology and narrative therapy I believe complement each other well. Central to this method is the consideration of power.[3]

LIBERATION IN THE FACE OF POWER

Common to Foucault's analysis of social power and liberation theologians' critique of Western industrialization is the understanding that the acquisition of wealth—whether in the form of intellectual or material capital—corrupts. Further, both agree that the attempts to pacify those who possess power result miserably in the continued oppression of the marginalized.

Even liberation of a people can result in further marginalization. African Americans in the United States have been liberated from the effects of segregation. However, their liberation has been acquired through Eurocentric approaches. For some African Americans, the result is an internalized colonization that cripples and minimizes (Akinyela 2008).

---

2. "Liberative," a term from Loren Townsend's *Introduction to Pastoral Counseling*, will be used to refer to a broad range of liberation theologies with the intent of recognizing oppressive structures and seeking methods of release from those structures.

3. Conversation, David Epston, Adelaide, South Australia, December 7, 2010. I discussed the connection of narrative therapy and liberation theology through power with David Epston. He thought it was promising to pursue recently having lectured in South America.

Further, true liberation from oppressive power also embraces access to spiritual richness as well as to "good enough" material goods. This liberation can be experienced by intentionally dismantling power. Freire's understanding of breaking through this cycle of power is through education of the populace. He contends that education in and of itself is not purely beneficent. Rather, it can liberate or oppress. His model connects with the common of life; observing; planning; acting; evaluating; replanning; and celebrating (Freire 2006).

A spiritually sensitive modification of Freire's work is seen in De La Torre's hermeneutical circle for ethics, with the addition of prayer. His method is as follows: (1) observing—historical and interpretive analysis; (2) reflecting—social analysis; (3) praying—theological and biblical analysis; (4) acting—implementation of praxis; (5) reassessing—new ethical perspectives; and then starting over (De La Torre 2004). This methodology lifts up the necessity of the spiritual, which is always a part of liberation theology but is sometimes overlooked.

LIBERATING STORIES OF THE SPIRIT

Lifting privilege and power from people's life stories is essential for thickening people's spiritual stories. Through prayer and reflection on the possibilities of one's spiritual narrative, a deepened faith story can occur. It will be a faith story that has been deconstructed in the face of oppressive dominant religious discourses as well as dominant cultural discourses.

Liberation theology has long held the image of Jesus as liberator of persons and stories by his opposition to oppressive political structures of his day. Jesus as liberator coauthors with us as we re-story those stories of faith. However, the work of the Spirit has long been ignored in theologies of all kinds. Long associated with an unhelpful dualism, a theology of the Spirit has too long focused on the ethereally spiritual divorced from the material world of earth and human.

Mary Grey, a feminist theologian, argues for revisioning the Holy Spirit in feminist terms. She focuses on a discourse of connection: "Every living system of the universe is interdependent and interconnected" (Grey 1991, 92). The image of the Spirit of God is seen as hovering over the earth and bringing to the world relational energy that is empathetic to all creation.

This feminine image of the Holy Spirit is in contrast to Congar and Boff's feminine images, which reinforce cultural gender stereotypes. Congar depicts the Holy Spirit as a mother who helps us get to know our father God and brother Jesus (Congar 1983a). Boff sees the Holy Spirit as being connected to

Mary, the mother of Jesus, and further elevates the feminine role of Mary, quite possibly continuing the cultural expectation of women to be mothers (Boff 1987).

A view of the Spirit compatible with feminist theology emphasizes inclusivity and relationality which breaks down capitalistic competition in favor of generosity. As the Spirit interacts with us, we become empowered to be renewed to new life (Poling 2011). Through this empowerment, we are liberated from oppressive structures.

So, from a liberating perspective, the Spirit is the Sustainer who uplifts people as they face difficult times. Through sustaining, the Spirit comforts and confronts people as they seek discernment through prayer. *Sustain* is a term used in narrative therapy to refer to stories and communities that support people during hard times. So, Spirit as Sustainer honors both narrative and liberation practices. Accessing the ascendant dimension of life through the Spirit offers a possibility of thickening stories of hope.

SPIRIT SUSTAINING THROUGH HOPE

Narrative re-storying encourages people to talk about their hopes and dreams. Reaching for hope is also rooted in liberation spirituality. For both narrative and liberative approaches, hope in the face of oppression only occurs in the here and now—rooted in real life. Yet, spirituality offers hope rooted in the ascendant and immanent of life, as well, I contend, as in the "material" of White's everyday, visible spirituality.

Standing in the present "material" world of this everyday spirituality, we are sustained by the Spirit as we look to the future. Several methodologies can serve us in this effort. We can accommodate to the current oppression; work for reforms; survive; rebel and overthrow oppression; or withdraw from our world (Poling 2011). Some of these choices can result in despair. Each choice may be necessary in different times.

Through re-storying of our spiritual narratives, we may be able to find power through ways in which the Spirit has sustained in past times when we were least aware. Our past painful experiences then become transformed into stories of faith that guide us toward the future. Companioning with us is the Spirit on that journey.

The Spirit offers liberating hope through connecting persons with their belief in God, others, and self by reminding us of the ways in which God is ever constant. Hope through the Spirit is connected with our past and present moving us toward the future so that at any time we participate in all three realms of time. The reality of narrative and liberative practices that contribute to re-storying our spiritual narratives comes through how we envision that task. To that task we now turn.

Practices

- Discuss in a small group your immediate responses when you hear the words *narrative, story,* and *liberation theology*. Reflect on ways in which your emotional response may differ from your intellectual response. Think about other theological perspectives that connect and/or challenge narrative practice.
- Reflect on the limitations and possibilities of narrative therapy and liberation theology as methods for deepening spiritual stories.

3

Pastoral Caring through Spiritual Narratives

Pastor Melissa wearily opened the door and put down her briefcase. She could still hear Mary's voice, "I just can't believe he's dead." Mark and Mary were a young couple in the congregation. Pastor Melissa had performed their wedding three years ago. Mark died quite unexpectedly from a heart attack. They had planned to start a family and now that dream was gone. The church was filled with church members mourning Mark's death. He was the youth group leader and a trustee. Now Pastor Melissa wondered how she could listen to Mary most fruitfully. How would she understand her faith stories in light of Mark's death? How should Mary talk with her?

Pastoral care often quietly listens to the grief of people having lost loved ones, confronts in the face of addictions, supports steadily when illness arrives. Pastoral care also celebrates with the start of coupled life, blesses new life, congratulates job promotions. The minister is privileged to join with people in their seasons of life through pastoral care.

Pastoral care occurs in many contexts. It sits on the front stoop of an East Coast city home. It talks in the church office of a pastor. It goes to the community room of a nursing home. It keeps a vigil in an intensive care unit of a hospital.

Pastoral care shines forth in many faces. It looks through the eyes of a hospital chaplain in a hospital emergency room. It shows on the face of a pastor counseling a premarital couple. It focuses through the glance of a minister working at community center for the homeless.

Pastoral care speaks through different words, dialects, and languages. It listens in various life transitions, difference places, and unique ministries of care. Yet it shares the common shape of story. Story has many different plots. The meaning that is conveyed through acts of pastoral care has the power to deepen faith. Discovering a story that is part of one's fabric of spiritual narratives can deepen faith more than pastoral care that does not explore such stories. We now turn our attention to the task of uncovering those spiritual narratives.

UNCOVERING SPIRITUAL NARRATIVES

In our previous discussions, we have identified some narrative and liberative practices that can be helpful in pastoral care and ministry. Power and hope emerge from narrative practice and liberation. Ministers can use these as questions in pastoral care to thicken the spiritual narratives of their church members both individually and collectively. How is power both a help and hindrance in those narratives? In what way can thickened stories lend hope as persons discover hopes and dreams in those spiritual narratives that have previously been undiscovered?

The beginning of uncovering spiritual narratives can be described as "a commitment to assisting people in reflecting upon the effects of internalized discourses that contribute to social injustice and maintenance of problem storying" (Duvall and Béres 2013, 205). The minister must be attentive to identifying what spiritual narratives may be blocking the careseeker's spiritual journey. Spiritual narratives, as previously defined, are those stories in one's life that give spiritual meaning through either an explicit belief system or an implicit spirituality that gives rise to spiritual beliefs that give meaning to life. They touch the vulnerable spirit of a careseeker. So, the minister must be sensitive to the sacred trust the person has given him or her.

A starting point for the minister in pastoral care is to establish a relationship with the careseeker that invites conversation in a mutual space. This role of the minister fits with the narrative position of the therapist as de-centered and influential (M. White 2005). In a similar way, the minister needs to take an inviting position that honors the careseeker as being most knowledgeable about his or her own life, while gently guiding the person to recognize those aspects of his or her story that they experience as most enriching.

As this relationship is developed, space is created for God's voice (Griffith and Griffith 2002). Thus, the sharing of the spiritual narrative that the careseeker[1] is most aware of will have tones of the voices of past religious leaders, Scripture, his or her voice, and voices of significant persons. Most importantly, the sacred space created holds God's voice. The way in which the

---

1. The term *careseeker* will be used in this book to refer to persons desiring pastoral care from a pastoral caregiver from Carrie Doehring's *The Practice of Pastoral Care: A Postmodern Approach* (2006).

storyteller encounters God's voice is critically important to how the spiritual narrative is experienced, told, and retold.

Spirituality practiced narratively from a pastoral care perspective invites the transcendent God to encounter the immanent human. This perspective is unique and contrasts with narrative practice in its natural form as expressed by Michael White when he stresses that spirituality of narrative practice is not to appeal to the divine but to "see and appreciate the visible in people's lives, and not the invisible" (2000b, 132).

White's quotation emphasizes the need for people to seek meaning in the everyday, common things of life, "little sacraments of daily existence" (2000b, 145) that bring meaning to people's lives. Such language used certainly has a spiritual nuance, yet does not fully invite a journey to "ascendant" or transcendent spirituality. Its critique seems to be that transcendent spirituality ignores the immanent or everyday aspects of human life. Nevertheless, White's narrative emphasis does not eliminate the possibility of a spirituality of the ascendant. A liberative narrative practice can, I believe, offer both immanent and ascendant spiritualities that enrich life.

Liberative narrative practice challenges the minister and careseeker to ground the storytelling in an awareness of justice for all people and recognition of the ways in which power and privilege can adversely impact the storying of faith. To this degree it is remarkably similar to narrative practice alone, as we have seen. However, it brings a further impact to the telling of spiritual narratives—that of centering hope in God and God's care of persons. Narrative, while talking about "hopes and dreams," anchors hope in relationships with others and causes of justice that are bigger than only individual humans. In addition to that narrative focus, I contend that believers look to God as the entity that is bigger than human concerns. By so doing, people can deepen their spiritual narratives. Through this joining of narrative and liberative practices, we continue in "breaking silences, urging prophetic action, and liberating the oppressed" (Miller-McLemore 2012, 250). Liberative narrative practice builds on that foundation to include God's care for humanity, embracing a hopefulness that mere human dreams cannot accomplish.

This pastoral task is not new. Two pastoral care images offer themselves as interesting containers of this process—Edward Wimberly's "indigenous storyteller" and Donald Capps's "agent of hope." Wimberly emphasizes the plot of the believer's story that correlates with the Christian story and posits that the dominant plot that gives meaning for the African American Christian is an eschatological one that envisions hope in the midst of suffering and oppression because God is working out God's purpose on behalf of persons. This, of course, echoes clearly the liberation theology in our earlier discussion. The purpose of the pastor as storyteller is to unfold, link, thicken, and twist the story in the context of God's story. Key to this process is the pastor's ability to help believers develop story language and story discernment. Further, Wimberly acknowledges the essential dimension of listening as well as telling the story (Wimberly 1997).

Capps's image of the minister is as an "agent of hope." His contention is that the pastor is unique among professionals in the ability to offer hope, which is a fragile commodity. Capps posits that for hope to occur, one must want hope, have desire for hope, and experience hope as a response to a felt deprivation (Dykstra 2005). Hope is primarily a form of perception that envisions a not-yet-existent future but brings those who hope to see the future as they would like it to be. Hope does not need to be tethered to only the realistic, but it needs to have some dimension that is close to a realizable possibility. Further, it needs to be connected to a personal and local context so it can be realized. Finally, two temporal aspects of hope—"future visioning" and "revising the past"—are important (Capps 1998).

A weaving of these two pastoral images seem to be possible as Andrew Lester draws some images to use in uncovering spiritual narratives in his *Hope in Pastoral Care and Counseling*. His eschatological understanding of hope is that humans are "multi-tensed" and need to experience hope in all the temporal dimensions. Further, Lester highlights narrative therapy as a psychotherapeutic approach that acknowledges the viability of hope in its practice (1995). I would propose a pastoral image of the minister as a "storyteller of hope." With this image, the minister is called to initially listen to the careseeker's story before responding with storytelling or guiding toward hope. The minister invites the careseeker to tell his or her story, and then he or she listens and tells the careseeker what is heard. In turn, the careseeker responds to the listening of the story. This is the narrative process of telling, retelling the telling, and retelling the retelling of the story.

EMBODYING AS STORYTELLER OF HOPE

How, then, does the minister embody the storyteller of hope in narrative ministry? The minister's personal and spiritual presence is the first stance of being a storyteller of hope. Pastoral presence as a critical component to caring is the foundation of pastoral literature historically. From Howard Clinebell's classic text *Basic Types of Pastoral Care and Counseling* to Doehring's *The Practice of Pastoral Care: A Postmodern Approach,* the minister must convey spiritual strength and compassion in order to merit the trust of careseekers. These qualities provide the relational framework for listening to people's stories.

Pastoral presence is more than just being with people. An unfortunate misunderstanding of pastoral presence from chaplaincy to congregational ministry sometimes sounds like, "I couldn't really do anything, but I was 'there' with the person." This frequently used sentence implies that some circumstances are so dire that a problem-solving approach is impossible. So the default position of "just" being there overshadows any possibility of active caring. Thickened pastoral presence through a narrative practice perspective embodies caring that is receptive to persons through active listening and spiritual direction.

Such pastoral presence eschews the pastoral caring that focuses on problem solving and vapid "presence" with careseekers. A narratively informed pastoral care perspective seeks to embody the storyteller of hope with some skills that enable the caregiver to provide a spiritually informed position. To be a storyteller of hope involves listening as well as telling the story back to the careseeker who tells a story. Hope here does not convey sheer hope devoid of any connection to a painful past or present. It is true to a liberation perspective that recognizes the pain of oppression from dominant discourses and experiences and that embraces the hopefulness that emerges from the dreams of the future that sustain people in the present.

Training in pastoral care courses as well as Clinical Pastoral Education in hospital settings emphasize the need to develop listening skills. Unfortunately, learning to listen involves attending to the words, body position, and voice of another. Other obstacles, such as over-identifying with the careseeker, can be examined through concepts such as "self of the pastor" or transference/ countertransference, depending on one's theoretical orientation of pastoral care.

The ability to listen to another also depends on an awareness of that which is sacred between the caregiver and careseeker, quite beyond sheer skills. Pastoral caregivers are uniquely qualified to attend to the sacred. Learning to listen in seminary and clinical settings can easily be distilled to psychological reflection and interpersonal skill building without taking seriously the spiritual gift of apprehending and attending to the spiritual in others' lives. Further, too little time in seminary and pastoral care training is focused on giving future caregivers "practice" in spiritual discernment.

The disciplines of pastoral care and spiritual formation have historically remained quite separate pastoral disciplines. In recent years, spiritual formation has been increasingly connected with pastoral care as evidenced by recent annual conferences of the Society for Pastoral Theology. Recent publications in pastoral care also distinguish spiritual care from pastoral care such as Bidwell's *Empowering Couple* (2013).

On the "secular" side, recognition of the importance of the sacred is seen in the growing "spiritual but not religious" designation in our society. Some of the data used to argue for the lessening of religion in the world is quite misleading. In the *Salt and Light* blog, the author emphasizes that still 80 percent of the world's population claims a specific religion and that at least 70 percent of the people polled who indicate they are nonreligious believe in God. So, we have a growing yearning for something, if not something religious, at least something spiritual (Boulton 2013). I experienced this in a storytelling workshop based on narrative practice. The workshop was focused on ways in which helping professionals can listen as well as tell stories that can foster increased engagement with others. The first exercise was to explore definitions of the term *sacred*. Participants were asked simply, "What does the word *sacred* mean to you?" ("Narativ 2-Day Listening and Storytelling Workshop for Helping Professionals" November 8 and 9, 2013).

Responses shared by the participants included descriptions of a sense of inclusion, meaning making beyond oneself, a sense of expansiveness, and more. I was the only person who included God in the definition, yet all the participants affirmed a general understanding and embracing of "sacred." Further, they understood stories to inhabit a sacred space. As pastoral caregivers, we need to be able to claim "sharing the sacred in story" as the central premise of our spiritual craft.

The storytelling methodology of Narativ, Inc. lends much to sharing the sacred in story between the pastoral caregiver and careseeker. Some of the organization's basic principles are as follows: (1) human beings are hardwired for story, (2) everybody has a story, (3) everybody can learn to tell their story, (4) everyone has a multiplicity of stories, (5) storytelling is everyone's access to creativity, and (6) there is a reciprocal relationship between listening and telling (Narativ, Inc. Handbook 2013, 3). All these principles are related to narrative practice as we have discussed. The value of these principles in embodying a storytelling of hope is that they are easy to practice as one responds to careseekers.

The last two principles of the Narativ, Inc. methodology offer some clear emphases that tease out some of the foundations of narrative therapy. An underlying assumption of narrative therapy is that uncovering one's stories can open up new experiences that result in empowered identities for people. However, the specific word *creativity* is not used in much narrative literature. As we seek ways to embody being a storyteller of hope, creativity offers possibilities for thickening the narrative practice of caregiving with a uniquely spiritual twist. I discuss below Narativ, Inc.'s reciprocity between listening and telling. Their creative dimension of narrative listening comes in a later chapter.

An earlier discussion contended that the idea of hope has not been fully developed in liberation theology. For liberation theologians, any future hope must be grounded in a present-day recognition of the oppressive discourses that affect careseekers. Yet, in times of trauma, people often cannot bear the pain of the present. They must look only to the future. It is often in the "sparkling" moment of the future that suffering believers can engage in the present.

Jesus as our liberator frees us both from oppressive social contexts as well as co-authors liberating stories that give us hope for the future. A storyteller of hope thus has the mission of recognizing present pain in the face of future hopes and dreams that have a spiritual source of sustenance. We pastoral caregivers are challenged to offer ourselves to others by recognizing the obstacles to listening that emerge. These obstacles may be external or environmental, physical or psychological, internal, meaning-making, or relational (Narativ, Inc. Handbook 2013).

These obstacles are contained in what we may envision as a "listening bowl" where we receive the stories of others and offer our listening to others. Contained in the bowl are all the obstacles that can block our listening. The receptivity of our listening shapes the way people tell their stories ("Narativ 2-Day Listening and Storytelling Workshop for Helping Professionals" November 8-9, 2013). In turn, then, we as pastoral caregivers respond to the story being told. Then, in reciprocity, the careseeker returns the story to us. This storying process follows the narrative methodology of telling, retelling the telling, and retelling the retelling.

Central to the embodiment of the storyteller of hope is the recognition that all caring is not only reciprocal but also emerges from relationships between ourselves and others through the Spirit. We receive care from others as we care for them as human vessels, becoming channels of blessing (Williams 1970). The caring from careseekers strengthens our connection with them and also our vulnerability, which can serve as an obstacle to authentic pastoral caring. We must be scrupulous in our own examination of spirit and psyche so that the Spirit may move through us.

This personal spiritual examination parallels the "de-centered and influential" position of the narrative practitioner. However, the embodiment of offering stories of hope is only sustained through an active process of caring. Pastoral care is known often through conversation. Conversations convey a different context than stories do. Stories have conversations, but a story conveys a notion of sustaining life. Narrative practice contends that a sacred space for stories can best be created through an active storying process.

Listening to Spiritual Narratives

Being a storyteller of hope means that listening and storytelling for the careseekers and caregivers inform each other on multiple levels. As a story is shared, underlying stories are there waiting to be uncovered. Sharing stories becomes a dynamic way to express pastoral caring in a contemporary culture of social media. Conversations can be ephemeral—gone with the click of "delete" on an e-mail or instant message. Writing down pastoral conversations in verbatim format has been a time-honored method for analyzing pastoral care interactions. The written words become expressions of the pastoral relationship. Jesus as the Word made flesh becomes alive in the actual speaking of words (Coyle 2007).

Pastoral conversations that encourage people to share their stories have often been framed in a more historical storyline. A careseeker typically comes to a caregiver with a problem-saturated story. The ways in which he or she experiences life, thoughts, feelings, and behaviors are overshadowed with a dominant story that blocks hope for the future. Pastoral care has often explored past stories with the assumption that "working through" the past will lead to insight that then leads to change.

Narrative pastoral care envisions changing problematic stories in quite a different way. A narrative pastoral care conversation will look for glimmers of new stories that can change the problematic stories. Then the emerging new story is extended into the future (Freedman and Combs 1996). By extending the story into the future, the problematic story remains as part of the careseeker's story but is also influenced for the better. The following is a helpful format for pastoral care conversations in a nonlinear narrative approach:

1. Begin with a unique outcome. Explore any experiences that the person has had that do not fit with the problematic story. For example, "Has there been a time when the depression did not overcome you?"
2. Make sure the unique outcomes represent a preferred experience. The careseeker will need to evaluate the unique outcomes. For example, "Was that experience a good one or bad one?"
3. Plot the story in the landscape of action. The "landscape of action" refers to the behaviors that are a background to the story. For

example, "How did you prepare yourself for that step? What exactly did you do?"

4. Plot the story in the landscape of identity. The "landscape of identity" refers to contributors to our identities as informed by our life stories. For example, "What does it say about you as a person that you would do this? What do you see in your relationship when you look at this event?" (Steps 3 and 4 can be woven back and forth.)

5. Ask about a past time that has something in common with the unique outcome or the meaning of the unique outcome. For example, "Were there times when you've done this kind of thing before? Who in your life would have predicted this event?"

6. Plot the story of the past event in the landscape of action, as in step 3.

7. Plot the story of the past event in the landscape of identity, as in step 4.

8. Ask questions to link the past episode with the present. For example, "Now that I understand its foundation in your past, do you see how this recent development in your relationship makes even more sense to you? When you think about that past time, does it put the experience that you had last week in a different light?" (Steps 3 through 8 facilitate the development of a history of the present.)

9. Ask questions to extend the story into the future. For example," Does looking at these events today have an impact on what you see in your future?" (Freedman and Combs 1996, 101-103)

While these steps have an implicit grounding in hope for the future, subsequent discussions of the *liberative* aspect of liberative narrative ministry will illumine the uniqueness of God sustaining us when human resources give way.

When reflecting on these steps in narrative pastoral care, one can see that "working through" past stories is clearly not the emphasis. This approach does not ask a careseeker to resolve the past; rather, it asks people to deconstruct stories whereupon future story development can be made. Misunderstandings can occur when talking about uncovering spiritual narratives. It can be misunderstood that one finds, as in an archaeological dig, a skeleton of a story that exists totally intact. Uncovering a spiritual narrative is more akin to a weaving process where the weaver reweaves a poorly woven portion of the tapestry into the new weaving.

Asking questions is an important skill that requires specialized training. The purpose of narrative questions is to generate experience rather than to gather information. The following are some questions intended to stimulate further possible questions:

- What conclusions about your relationship have you drawn because of this problem?
- Does this situation that you describe encourage particular feelings in your life?
- How were you recruited into this way of thinking?
- Are there places where it is more likely you'll be pulled into drinking?
- What are the effects on your life of this belief that you are not a good person?
- How has this pattern influenced other family members?
- Are there other problems that depression teams up with?
- What does this idea have you doing?
- What ideas, habits, and feelings feed the problem?
- What ways of life does racism (or other oppressive cultural discourse) ride piggyback on?
- Have there been times when arguing could have taken control but didn't?
- What does this new perspective tell you about yourself?
- Why does this new way of thinking suit you better than the old way? (Freedman and Combs 1996)

These types of questions can find themselves accompanying the development of a story of spiritual narratives as deconstruction weaves different elements of the story together. Two of the most helpful approaches identified in earlier chapters for a narrative pastoral care conversation—externalization and unique outcomes—are evident in a transcript of a pastoral care conversation I had with a careseeker who came to me for a few sessions of pastoral conversation.

Yvonne was a thirty-year-old white female, single with no children. The presenting concern was her conflict with coworkers on the job. Yvonne reported that sometimes she "just got mad at people at work for no reason." Yvonne was the only daughter of a single-parent family with three older brothers. Her mother and father divorced when she was quite young. Yvonne's mother "never had good relationships with men." Yvonne did not have a relationship with her father when growing up. Now she was trying to establish a relationship with him. Her family history was emotionally and physically abusive. Yvonne's brothers often hit her while her mother was at work.

The following transcript takes a segment of my pastoral care conversation with Yvonne that illustrates the narrative practice of externalizing. The comments indicate my intent in the conversation and places where I would want to do better.

S: We talked about your wanting to work on anger. So, I've been thinking about some questions to ask you about that. I'd like to ask you some questions that I hope will be helpful about anger and you can let me know if they're helpful.

Positioning therapist to be collaborative

Y: OK.

S: Anger is your big concern. So I wondered if it would be helpful for you to reflect on when anger first became a big part of your life.

Externalizing question—should have focused on question format

Y: Umm. . . . I guess when I was little.

S: OK, so do you remember much about that time with anger?

Y: Well, I didn't know much about anger. I guess it came from all the trauma with my siblings. I didn't think much about it until later when I started to get in trouble with the law and at school.

"Getting into trouble" could be another externalization? Effects of problem

S: How did that affect you at school?

Y: Well, I fought a lot. I was defiant. I drank, I smoked. I guess kind of a typical teenage phase.

S: Did the anger show up at particular times when you look back upon it?

Should have left off "the" and used "anger"

Y: Yes, now that I know, I would say it happened because I didn't know how to express my feelings. I know I became physical because I didn't know how to communicate my feelings. I didn't know what to do, so it would just build up and build up.

S: So it sounds like you had a difficult time when you were growing up when your siblings actually physically abused you. It sounds like all those feelings about their abusing you got all bottled up inside. So that you would actually . . . let me back up. So, I'm wondering if you were actually surprised when the anger came on and overtook you. Or were there some things you missed when anger would show up?

Y: Well, I would be surprised. Or let me say that I would be surprised at how I expressed anger. So I would get angry but it was the extreme to which I would release it.

S: So, it sounds like you were able to look ahead . . . to know when anger was having an effect on you. *Helpful move to focus on effects of problem*

Y: It was like a fight or flight. It was like that [snaps fingers].

S: What kind of impact did it have on you at that time?

Y: I didn't know it then. But, now that I'm older, I was scared, accused. It would come on . . . all kind of mixed emotion. I would regret it.

S: So as you describe it, there was a whole flurry of other feelings, that would leave you feeling angry, confused. You said it was quick! That it would come upon and you would have a sense of regret.

Y: Afterwards. . . .

S: So now as you look back on the anger, what are some of effects you see? You mentioned regret. So, I'm wondering as you look back on it, what are some of the effects?

Y: As I got older, I realized I didn't know how much I could take. When I got in trouble with the law, I realized I had to get it out in some way, through therapy.

S: So as you describe anger then, how would you describe the impact of anger today? *Focusing on landscape of events—future perspective*

Y: When I learned when I work with the kids at my job that anger is an emotion that everyone has. It's how you learn to channel it.

S: So, things . . . Let me back up. So, now what has enabled you to look at anger differently now than perhaps the way you did several years ago?

Y: Yes . . .

S: Yes, it sounds like even though you've had a struggle with anger all your life, that things are more different now than then. That maybe now you're *Moving toward re-authoring or re-storying* looking at anger in a different way. It strikes me that may have been something within you and your story that has changed a bit to enable you to look at anger differently when it comes your way. And I'd be interested in what your thoughts are about that.

Y: It's arrived differently with counseling and getting in trouble . . .

S: The consequences . . .

Y: Yeah, the consequences. . . . I think just life . . .

S: Yeah, that can be. Just growing up. . . . You mentioned about being in trouble with the law. What kind of effect did anger have upon you in the legal system. It sounds like what you're saying is that it got you in trouble with the law. What do you think about that?

Y: As far as anger, I got possession of a handgun. I don't know if I would have used it. But the way my anger got out of control, I might have.

S: As you describe that, it sounds like . . . Let me   Effects
back up. . . . I'm really kind of interested in the
impact of anger upon your whole life. I'm
wondering if it's something you always felt you had
to fight against . . . something that kind of sneaks up
behind you and something that surprises you . . . that
scares you.

Y: It was when I was younger. The older I get with   Prayer as re-
counseling the better able I am to control it. I   authoring or re-
channel it in a different way, walk away, that things   storying—thickening
that irritate me. Prayer has a lot to do with it.   the story

S: I'd be interested more in how prayer helps you battle anger.

Y: Well, I joined church in 2000 and it seemed like another outlet for me. Walking away, playing basketball, talking with someone. . . . I can pray. I didn't feel like I had to worry about getting anger triggered . . . that I was in a safe haven.

S: Alright. . . . Well, you mention the words, "safe   "Safe haven" is
haven." Wow, that's a pretty powerful statement.   another
Reminds me of some gospel hymns. And what   externalization that
enables you to be in that safe haven?   helps in re-
authoring or re-
storying

Y: My mind kind of plays with things. Like the devil saying, "You don't fit in here, you don't fit in there." I can have the will that I want to go [to church] and that I need to go.

S: So, actually getting to church is a big feat. What you're saying is that at times it feels like the devil tempts you. Is that what you mean? That the devil puts obstacles in your way about getting to church. During those times when you feel like you're tempted, what's been helpful for you?

Y: I pray always and then I think about how church helps me, helps me fight the devil. I find something there. . . And then I think about what might happen if I don't go and find that safety.

S: You think about the consequences? You think about church being a safe haven, overcoming your temptation. I don't know, maybe you're . . .

Yvonne's problem-saturated story is focused around anger and how its effects have caused many dilemmas in her life. By externalizing her anger, she is able to look at what kind of effects anger has on her and her life. Yvonne then talks about joining church and the difference it has made in her life. I lift up the phrase "safe haven" because it seems to offer the possibility of a unique outcome for her. Thus, the words "safe haven" function as a gateway to a new story of hope. As the conversation continues, we thicken the phrase as it becomes a counterstory to the story of anger's effects on her.

LISTENING TO SPIRITUAL NARRATIVES OF FAMILIES

Listening to families as a storyteller of hope uses the same types of questions and same approach as with individuals. A basic approach is to externalize the problem story of the family and then look for unique outcomes. One difference in working with families is that the person engaging in pastoral care should work with the family to identify a narrative that affects the entire family—a story that is shared by all family members (Coyle, in press).

Let us meet a family with a presenting concern to see how listening to that family and offering hope might occur. John, age forty, and Sarah, age forty, have two children, Megan, age fifteen, and Jason, age thirteen. The Smiths are active members of your congregation. They come to you in distress because

Megan is anorexic. You know that you will refer the family to a family therapist who is skilled in treating eating disorders. At the same time, you can offer a pastoral care conversation to the Smiths as their pastor.

The Smiths express their pain of how the whole family is fearful for Megan's life. They describe the extreme measures they take to ensure her safety. Jason glumly says that "everything is about Megan." Sarah says that despite trying to do all the right things, nothing seems to help. John expresses his sense of helplessness. Sarah says nothing.

Your first step is to externalize anorexia. You say, "What happens when anorexia enters the family room?" A lively conversation begins that lifts up the effects of anorexia on the entire family. At one point, Sarah says, "We pray constantly for Megan and try to be faithful. All the right things don't work."

At this point, stories of anorexia and being a faithful Christian emerge. The family reports the crippling pain of seeing Megan deteriorate while believing that their faith does not have a salvific effect on the dilemma. The next step for you would be to inquire of the family whether they have had the experience of prayer having a beneficial effect on a problem. Then you begin to weave that story of experience with the current dilemma.

As the stories are uncovered, you explore with the family ways in which the unique outcome of a beneficial story of prayer may impact their current dilemma. During this conversation, the family begins to experience something hopeful about how things may or may not develop in addressing the anorexia. They begin to talk about how their life as a family never counts on prayer except when they want a miracle. A rich spiritual conversation emerges. You agree to talk with them periodically while they see a family therapist, limiting your role to pastor.

One can see from these examples of a storyteller of hope listening with the careseekers to ways in which spiritual narratives can honor being with others in pain while at the same time lifting up hope. Further, we have illustrated the narrative "de-centered but influential" position of the pastor. Finally, the clear voice of liberation theology is heard as efforts are made on the part of the careseekers and caregiver to join with hope. Future discussions will highlight the social justice element of liberation theology that is expressed in liberative narrative therapy.

PRACTICES

- Create a group of three persons—storyteller, story listener, and story observer. Each person will take five minutes to tell a common story. Rotate until all persons have had a turn at each of the roles. The storyteller is to focus on a rich description, including all the senses, of some place he or she visited that was quite pleasant. The story listener is to listen to what is said, not to interpret the story, and then should repeat back the story to the storyteller. The story observer is available for assistance, then, with no normative critique, comments on the process to all when the storying is finished.

4

Narratively Ministering to Congregations and Communities

Contemporary congregations and community ministries run the gamut from those that do not seem to have left the stereotypical 1950s to communities that seem never to use the words *Jesus* or even *God* in their mission statements. Determining what a congregation or ministry is can even be difficult. The growing pluralism and multiculturalism in our society has broadened the criteria for community ministries that qualify as nonprofit organizations. "Spiritual but not religious" joins the list of denominations and faiths that qualify as nonprofit organizations.

These multiple and sometimes conflicting definitions of faith can be seen more broadly in the loosely postmodern milieu of our society. The large metanarratives of culture that once held society together seem random and at best uncertain. In a world where mass shootings and terrorism occur with regularity, humans yearn for some stability. In light of this, we all may hope for a faith that responds to our life journeys in the light of God's sustaining love for us.

Both inflexible and overly inclusive statements of faith may fail to sustain our faith development. In addition, communities of faith ranging from a diocesan cathedral to a house church may falter by offering either too rigid a structure where change is not honored or too fluid a context where stability is not honored.

We may encounter either rigidity or diffuseness as we move in our faith development. Both possibilities may block the deepening of our spiritual narratives as we grow in faith. Fear of failure or pain may limit our risking growth. But, perhaps, if we are able to find a safer transition zone, we can move into the future. Narrative practice's scaffolding, I believe, offers such a transition for us.

Scaffolding, a narrative practice, honors the journey between "what is known and familiar and what might be possible for people to know about their lives" (M. White 2007, 263). In short, it is a way in which the therapist, pastor, or community director can assist a person to take short steps toward future possibilities. Undoubtedly, sometimes we will turn around and walk back to the past before moving forward. As noted in our previous discussion, scaffolding enables careseekers to find common elements of the known in the unknown so they move forward with less fear.

This narrative practice offers much for those persons who would like to "narratively" lead congregations and ministries. By listening to cues from fellow travelers, pastoral leaders can look both to histories of spiritual practices as well as to the hopes and dreams of the future. This process, I believe, can center itself in using story in ministry through the support of narrative practices. We now turn to examine ways to narratively lead, teach, and worship through practices that resist, empower, nurture, and liberate (Miller-McLemore 2012).

NARRATIVELY LEADING

The phrase "narratively leading" is actually a misnomer when considering its narrative context. Narrative practice looks at the role of the therapist as being "de-centered and influential" in relationship to the client. Thus, the therapist is not the expert in matters of the therapy process since the client is viewed as being the expert of his or her own life. Neither is the therapist merely a sounding board of either transferential relationships or words from the client. Narrative practitioners see the therapist as that person who enables the client to share life stories and coedits those stories by lifting up the thin threads of story that the client may ignore or not be aware of.

Further, this stance of the therapist is distinctly in relationship to the client. In fact, one of the maps that can guide narrative therapy is called a *statement of position* in which the therapist makes decisions about how to "position" himself or herself in relationship to the client. In this position, the therapist deliberates about what questions to ask and how to leverage the client's uncovered stories has so that his or her life story can be thickened.

Ministry studies have historically called the vocation of pastoral leadership "church administration" or "church leadership." The first term evokes a more traditional leadership style in which the pastoral leader oversees or manages the church in a style akin to corporate leadership, inviting reflection on whether church administration should be an application of business management. The second term conveys a pastoral role of leading rather than administering. This latter term connects better with traditional images of the pastor as shepherd rather than as business leader. It also offers the possibility of sharing the leadership with laity.

Such sharing of leadership sometimes disintegrates into encouraging laity to do everything in the church, often without providing them any specific training, and into involving—as the bulletin epithet says—'Ministers: Everyone." Certainly, in a congregation or community ministry responsibility needs to rest with someone. And lay ministry is a vital part of congregational life.

Seward Hiltner's perspectival approach focuses on administering, communicating, and healing as critical aspects of ministry (1958). This approach used field theory, an emerging theory at the time, to ground the function of the pastor in the congregation. Shepherding thus became revitalized as a pastoral image that had biblical links and that offered some flexibility in how a pastoral leader envisioned his or her work.

The pastoral images of agent of hope and indigenous storyteller, described in an earlier chapter, can perhaps be helpfully used with Hiltner's approach when focusing on the stance of the pastoral leader as a storyteller of hope. The blending of the two pastoral images—shepherd and storyteller of hope—also works well with the narrative therapist being "de-centered and influential." The storyteller of hope offers an empowering presence that can be used in various pastoral roles—even as a spiritual practice leader as seen in the Staff of Spirit in the next chapter.

Recent ministerial literature focusing on church leadership used Bowen theory to lift up the function of the pastoral leader. The pastor in a Bowenian approach is to be a well-differentiated leader. As a result, a deluge of ministry literature focusing on being well differentiated was published. Then, Bowen family theory, also known as Bowen family systems, came to be referred to as family systems theory in most pastoral ministry literature. Other family systems approaches are hardly mentioned. The assumption has become that family systems theory is automatically Bowen theory.

I must admit that I see the model of differentiated leadership to have some serious limitations that are rarely acknowledged. The Bowen model of differentiation was originally applied to the role of the therapist as coach in working with clients. Bowen training emphasizes that the therapist be aware of the limitations that his or her family of origin has on work with clients. Behind that assumption is the likelihood that the therapist of Bowenian inclination is in personal therapy, has had personal therapy, or is participating in some clinical consultation group.[1] While this is theoretically helpful, I suspect that the average minister is not actively engaged in therapy or even in a clergy peer group.

Further, some structural problems exist with a pastor being able to be differentiated and non-anxious in a congregation. Particularly in congregations with local church autonomy, the distance between the pulpit and out the door can be very short. Depending on a congregation for sustenance always raises anxiety. Thus, I often change the phrase from "non-anxious" to "less anxious."

The Bowenian model of differentiated leadership espouses the ability of the leader to move ahead of the congregation while remaining connected with the congregation. While an admirable achievement, it is an extremely difficult reality to attain. Also, I have experienced the extreme of such leadership where pastors mistakenly misunderstand the true concept of differentiation. Sometimes pastoral leaders act with emotional indifference to persons in the community of faith instead of processing feelings before reacting impulsively. The result can be that congregants experience a sense of not being cared for by their pastoral leader.

In recent years, narrative approaches have illumined ministry studies. "Narrative"—which is clearly not a copyrighted word—has been used in multiple meanings. Mostly, narrative refers to telling a story in a linear plot; unfortunately, this is often done with the understanding that there is just one story. The Narrative Leadership Collection of the Alban Institute, following a recent trend in ministry literature, grounds much of its writing on the strong theoretical foundations of different approaches to narrative thinking, which includes the narrative therapy of White and Epston. No specific narrative approach to leadership is offered, however, that can be applied to different contexts of ministry. Using story as discussed in this book can open some paths for using a narrative therapy approach as seen through a pastoral care narrative perspective.

The use of story in pastoral leadership helps expand the concept of ministry to include community leaders along with pastors and religious leaders. Storying thickens the meaning making of both individual and collective stories in that faith community. It encourages a participatory approach in faith communities that is essential for spiritual vibrancy: "A participatory approach to pastoral practice acknowledges the tension between doctrine and our lived reality and invites active, collaborative reflection on the effects of our theological meaning-making" (Barker 2010, 50).

1. Edwin Friedman's *Generation to Generation: Family Process in Church and Synagogue* presented Bowen theory applied in a compelling way to communities of faith. Other authors who followed in Bowenian pastoral applications include Peter Steinke and Ron Richardson.

This pastoral narrative practice suggested for such leadership includes (1) naming the voices, (2) exploring the effects of the voices, and (3) questioning the "truth" claims of the voices (Barker 2010). These suggestions for pastoral practice can be used through story as the minister facilitates the storytelling. A thread that emerges in extant literature on narrative leadership is the idea that the pastor should be able to share his or her story with the congregation. Hester and Walker-Jones talk about this model as they practiced it with a clergy peer group (Hester and Walker-Jones 2009). Their peer group model is quite true to White and Epston's narrative approach. Further, it offers a clear distinction from other models that emphasize the pastor sharing his or her story, but that the community of believers are not to model their stories after the pastor's story.

These practice steps would not "privilege" the pastoral leader's story. Rather, members of the community would be invited to share their stories as well as the minister's story to illustrate Friere's rich statement of "unity through diversity." A collective narrative process that has been described in previous chapters could be used to build a sense of unity in a community of believers before conflict strikes. It is usually at those times of conflict that a congregation calls for "good leadership," whatever that may mean. Thus, my suggested narrative approach could serve to develop cohesiveness with the believers.

Interestingly enough, some pastoral leadership approaches that do use a narrative approach based on White and Epston also assume that family systems and narrative naturally go together (Golemon 2010b; Savage and Presnell 2008). However, narrative therapy does not use systems theory as a theoretical foundation, rather it uses anthropology, social construction, and Foucauldian postmodernism. Jill Freedman once commented that narrative therapy, while not systemic, found a home in family therapy (Freedman 2010). Narrative therapy is family therapy that is not a systems based approach. The method of each is different; family systems approaches emphasize recurring patterns while narrative therapy emphasizes interwoven layers.

The interweaving of layers of stories—the re-storying—strengthens a community of faith and sustains them in hard times. Thus, the storyteller of hope needs to invite all the voices of the faith stories to be spoken in order to explore the effects of those stories on the lives of believers as well as on spiritual beliefs that people have to come accept as true. Taking a non-expert stance evokes the ethos of liberation theology. This process is similar to engaging in postcolonial analysis. Members of a community are encouraged to resist having meaning making imposed them. They are then enabled to create their own context of belief (Akinyela 2002).

Telling stories, retelling stories, and retelling stories in narrative practice do not solve problems alone. However, they do thicken the spiritual narratives of a community, enabling it to be more resilient to trauma. "Congregational stories are narrated practices" that enable a community of faith to share a common spiritual experience (Shapiro 2010, 100).

Those seeking to narratively lead a congregation, chaplaincy department, pastoral counseling center, or community organization can use these narrative practices by first becoming storytellers of hope. A critical first step, this sets the tone for employing the practices just discussed. A case study will now illustrate implementing these practices. All identifying information has been changed.

Case Study of Narratively Leading

Grace Community Church called Beth as pastor after a period of conflict. The church had closed for a few years and then was reopened as a "restart" church by its denomination. Grace Church was located in a rural area that was experiencing some new growth. The hope was that new residents in the community might mean new members for the church.

It was surprising that the church called Beth as pastor since she was the first female minister in the county. However, a prominent family in the church immediately connected with her. They became quite influential in her calling. Things went really well for a period of time. Some members were added. The congregation seemed content.

Then, old conflicts arose. Divisions began to grow in the congregation. At first, Beth decided to focus more on the emotional system of the congregation and become a well-differentiated pastor. However, despite her own therapy, the gnawing in her stomach voiced that differentiation was indeed difficult. Further, she found that her attempts to distance herself from the conflict were viewed by the congregation as indifference.

Then, a surprising idea overtook Beth. She knew that the members of the congregation loved telling stories. The women were also expert quilt makers. So, she developed a storytelling circle to share stories of the painful and joyful history of the congregation. People shared stories that had not been told for generations. Each family made quilt squares to illustrate their family's connection with the congregation. The women's quilting circle made a quilt telling the spiritual narratives of the church that was hung in the sanctuary.

Conflicts did not evaporate. However, the congregation was able to move forward as it became united in its diversity. Beth, as a storyteller of hope, was able to modify the narrative practice of outsider witnesses, to insider witnesses who were church members. The members were able to tell their stories.

Beth also used scaffolding as she carefully listened to the congregants—holding their stories until they were able to take further steps. As they ventured into the future, their fear dissipated and they become more hopeful.

The quilting became a variation of the narrative practice of sending letters to those who experience trauma. Those who were the recipients of the "letter" were fellow church members as they created their own "letters" of quilt squares that served as reminders in the sanctuary of their shared spiritual narratives.

NARRATIVELY TEACHING

Naming of the church's ministry of teaching takes many forms. The term *Christian education* is largely used in extant literature, *religious education* is used in some contexts, and *Christian formation* in other contexts. All these terms indicate a dimension of ministry in the church that takes its primary focus to be teaching believers to study the Bible, to learn the tenets of the faith, and to practice their faith. In all of these aspects, the ministry of Christian education is an ongoing process. It moves forward toward the future.

So, to reflect the dynamic direction of Christian education, the concept of teaching faith will be used to describe a liberative narrative practice that lifts up the histories of faith so that the future may be sustained for future believers. Teaching faith involves both teacher and learner in a circular process that calls forth caring and liberating qualities of all participants. Such a participatory process requires some foundation that lends itself to dynamic learning. The theoretical foundations of Lev Vygotsky and Paulo Freire lend themselves to be woven with narrative practice and liberation theology for such a process.

Recent narrative practice uses the work of Russian psychologist Lev Vygotsky through the concepts of the *zone of proximal development* and *scaffolding*. Vygotsky developed these concepts through his interest in early childhood learning. The prevailing developmental theories at that time were threefold: development always precedes learning, learning and development are occurring simultaneously, and learning and development are separate but interactive processes. Vygotsky countered these understandings with the premise that learning always precedes development and requires the assistance of a mentor. He further emphasized that learning was not the product of individual effort but of social collaboration (Vygotsky 1986).

As children came to be mentored by adults, the movement to a place of learning was referred to as the zone of proximal development. This zone is the distance between what a child knows independently and what is possible to learn in collaboration with others. Bridging the gap requires that the learning process be broken down into manageable blocks where an available mentor can assist in the movement. Vygotsky called this process "scaffolding" (M. White 2007).

As the child moves across the zone of proximal development, a shift occurs from gathering the objects and events of the world under a common name to gathering the objects and events of the world into chains of associations that establish a relationship between these objects and events. This process enables the child to be able to shape his or her own actions in constructing his or her own life. This leads to what narrative practitioners would call "personal agency" (M. White 2007).

The implications of Vygotsky's ideas are rich indeed for narrative practice. The stance of the narrative practitioner as "de-centered and influential" fits well within this mode. As the careseeker works to uncover stories, the practitioner allows for the agency of the person to develop and can offer helpful assistance when appropriate. It evokes the image of two fellow travelers where one has hiking experiencing and the other has none. The journey is from a familiar place to one that is unknown yet possible to know. Along the journey both seasoned traveler and novice consult with other travelers to determine the most opportune path.

Social collaboration, which is a critical part of Vygotsky's thinking, connects well with Freire's notion of education that starts from the bottom up and his recognizing the essential need to consult with those people who are the focus of the education. Freire argues that the context of learning should occur where the people live (Freire 1994).

Education can be based on an elitist notion in which the teacher determines which knowledge one needs to know, regardless of its fit with the learner. This approach fails because people who do not live in the same culture as the academically elite are not transforming their life experience as part of their education. The result is that the native knowledges of the people's culture are viewed as inferior to the knowledges of the teacher and academia. Further, the learning does not integrate the richness of the learner's life stories.

A believer's life stories can be viewed through the creation of spiritual narratives. Freire writes, "This is how I have always understood God—a presence in history that does not preclude me from making history, but rather pushes me toward world transformation, which makes it possible to restore the humanity of those who exploit and of the weak" (Freire 1997, 103–4). Liberative narrative practice involves lifting oppression from the oppressed but also engaging those who oppress by exploring their histories and using them to see themselves through the lens of the oppressed.

Having examined some primary concepts of Vygotsky and Freire, I now turn to some suggestions about narratively teaching through a liberative narrative perspective. Both these thinkers focus on the necessity of a rich collaborative community for learning. Golemon echoes this emphasis as he stresses the importance for narrative leaders to evoke stories in their congregations that are "collaborative and intentional" (2010c, 17). Further, he states that "reconstructive narratives appeal to canonical understandings of tradition and practice but they invite the canon's disruption and renegotiation as a sign of the tradition's vitality" (19).

Liberative narrative teaching then demands that the appropriating of the Bible and Christian traditions be grounded contextually in the believer's faith community where others can both support and challenge the integration of Christian belief with the believer's own spiritual narratives and life. Individual stories are honored as they are viewed in the tapestry of other believers' stories, finally arriving at a rich thickening of the congregation's faith story. At the same time, God's story as revealed in the Bible is always the dominant story by which all stories are interpreted.

This does not mean, however, that God's involvement in our own spiritual narratives is rigidly interpreted. Kathryn Hoffman (2010) describes a project of contextual learning that involved seminary students in the role of "story brokers" in which they pay attention to what's happening, evoke the stories of what is happening, listen carefully to what and how the stories are told, gather and interlace these stories with the biblical story, discern a preferred, emerging story, and tell that preferred story.

In the project, students were assigned to a different cultural context outside of the church such as a YMCA, pub, or coffeehouse. Following the guidelines for story brokering described above, the students were to imagine how the persons they engaged in this out of the church context might connect with aspects of stories from the Gospels in their Gospels class. The interweaving of the personal stories with the biblical story thickened the students' own stories as they were interwoven with multiple stories. The challenge for the students was to keep their learning "storied," which meant that they looked for interconnecting narratives that might give them clues for interpretation (Hoffman 2010).

Interpretation becomes a challenge for liberative narrative teaching. Study of biblical texts always involves some type of interpretation, which may vary widely. At the same time, liberative narrative teaching requires that the storyteller or believer is the expert on his or her story. How then do we keep our own spiritual narratives while seeking for God in the biblical text?

The believer needs to identify those hermeneutical principles that best support his or her view of biblical interpretation. Weaving personal spiritual narratives with the biblical witness becomes a critical factor. Identifying such spiritual narratives can come through a practice of identifying significant spiritual experiences and expanding those experiences so they can scaffold one's emerging spiritual narrative through a re-storying process (Coyle 2013).

Liberative narrative teaching at this point engages with the believer's community of faith. Sharing participants' spiritual narratives prior to studying the biblical text is critical. Here each person shares his or her most formative spiritual narrative. The text is then studied with the witness of preferred hermeneutical principles as participants tell their stories and others retell their stories. Salient points of the biblical text are told as they resonate with the retelling of the stories known in narrative practice as retelling the retelling. Thus, the storytelling unfolds in the context of God's story for all people.

Christian formation, which emphasizes deepening of spiritual experiences so that practicing Christian faith is a natural development of studying Christian beliefs, is related to liberative narrative teaching. At the same time, this function of faith is also related to pastoral caring through nurturing the believer to grow in faith. Caring from a trusted guide is one way that believers may develop a more mature faith. An example of how this may occur is illustrated in the following case study. Identifying information has been changed.

Case Study of Narratively Teaching

Evan was called to a large community church as minister to young adults. A recent seminary graduate, he was excited about his new calling. At first, things went well. His outgoing personality was a good fit for the lively congregation.

The first Bible study he led was a success. He followed the curriculum that the senior minister had suggested. The participants expressed their satisfaction with the material. The group began to grow. These young adult members were originally members of the congregation who connected strongly with the senior minister under whose leadership they had been children and teens.

However, a good problem developed. New members came to the Bible study attracted by the church's public appeal and use of media. Their theological beliefs were quite different from that of the senior minister, the original young adult members, and the rest of the congregation. Evan had a challenge. He wanted to attract a diverse group of people. However, the diversity also included theological diversity. Evan seemed baffled. Then, he began to think like a narratively influenced teacher.

Evan continued to use the same curriculum. However, he began to use the curriculum in a new way. He developed a Vygotsky-influenced approach to developmental learning. Instead of focusing the Bible study on the material itself, he focused the learning on developing mentoring relationships. Pairing older members with younger members enabled the participants to discuss the material less defensively.

Further, he included awareness from Freire in the Bible study. As the material was studied, Evan created a variety of voices who would respond to the material—an unemployed single mother, a disabled Iraq veteran, a family whose home had been foreclosed. Each voice responded to the material in the way the individual thought a person in that role would have. Then, the group grounded the Bible in the present through addressing community needs as an extension of their study. In this narrative teaching, multiple voices are invited to the discussion. Learning occurs as seasoned Bible study members provide scaffolding to take new members further into the discussion. As this process continues, members gradually let go of fear and embrace hope. At the same time, the social context of narrative practice joins with the Freirean approach to create social change from the bottom up and not from a hierarchical edict of a leader.

Narratively Worshipping

Worshipping is a central focus of any ministry. Believers come to engage with each other and to worship God. Prayer, liturgy, music, preaching, and witnessing all come together to focus on individual and collective spiritual narratives of the congregation. The central focus of Christian worship is the sermon that seeks to engage God's story with believers.

Narrative preaching is currently understood through two approaches (Allen, e-mail, September 27, 2013). The first approach understands the sermon to be a story. One method of applying this approach is to create a sermon that is an actual story—setting, plot, and characters. No moral is usually drawn. The preacher allows the sermon in story form to speak for itself. A more nuanced way of understanding the sermon as a story comes through its literary structure. It has a definite starting point and moves toward a destination. Along the way the sermon uses stories, biblical exegesis, reflection, news stories, and more. Another method is the first person sermon. It is a story in terms of its movement, not its content.

A recent narrative preaching approach is based on a postmodern sensibility (Allen 2008). In this view, preaching's mission is to read the Bible as a narrative that shapes the identity of the church. The preacher does not try to make a case for the claims of the Bible or to revise the Bible in terms of what would be acceptable to today's listeners. The purpose of the sermon in this approach is to narrate the church as a continuation of the narrative begun in the Bible.

Liberative narrative preaching has some commonalities with these approaches as well as some differences. The structure of the sermon itself is less important than its method. And its movement is designed to evoke questions on the part of the listeners as well as to generate a new experience. Both of these goals then thicken the spiritual narratives of believers.

This narrative preaching understands the sermon is a story. Its structure can be an actual story or not. But, it does have the movement at all times of a story in that its structure will tell events or components that share a plotline over time (Craddock 2008). Further, its purpose is to connect the landscape of events, as described in narrative practice, with a landscape of identity. Telling the events is not enough; rather, one must ensure that the listener makes meaning of those events so they thicken the spiritual narratives that form the believer's identity of faith.

Liberative narrative preaching shares with the second postmodern narrative approach a recognition that our culture is largely lacking metanarratives that are accepted without question and lend stability in society. Simultaneously, it does not share the theological certainty of the Bible's witness. That determination is left to the believer so that his or her hermeneutical preferences are honored at all times, just as narrative practitioners privilege a person's preferred story.

At this point, liberative narrative preaching diverges from both approaches to narrative preaching. It embraces the three methods of inquiry in narrative practice[2] that contribute to a restoried account of people's spiritual narratives as they listen to the sermon. First, it is rooted in a political line of inquiry. "Political" here refers to narrative practice's belief that all individual struggles or problems represent a social issue. In this preaching, such political inquiry is grounded in a liberation theology ethos that recognizes the need to embed

---

2. David Epston identified three methods of inquiry—political, ethical, and poetic—at a workshop at Evanston Family Therapy Center.

future hope within simultaneous struggles to change dominant cultural and socioeconomic discourses.

Preaching with political inquiry assumes that all spiritual challenges are both individual and collective, grounded in one's social location as well as being connected to the retelling of the spiritual narrative with an eye to the issues of the local congregation. To use a common idiom, liberative narrative preachers regularly "quit preaching and go to meddling." However, this preaching does not offer a normative political or spiritual viewpoint because the listener with God is the authority on his or her own faith stance. The sermon thus has a direct application to the life of the community where the preaching occurs. It is political.

The second line of inquiry focuses on ethics. This inquiry does not limit itself to an understanding of ethical inquiry as concerning only moral judgments of right or wrong. Ethical inquiry is concerned with the privileging of dominant cultural discourses that can be oppressive. It also calls narrative practitioners to be respectful, always taking care with their position of power with their clients. This means that they are always careful to consider the impact of their presence in the life of the clients.

This is also true with liberative narrative preaching. The preacher is always mindful that the pulpit belongs to the people and God. He or she is an honored guest. Thus, the utmost hospitality is shown to the listeners. This does not mean, however, that honest preaching is not important. To attempt to make comments that ingratiate the preacher in the lives of the listeners is an ultimate ethical transgression. Further, the hope that must be present in liberative preaching cannot coexist with false reassurance. Ethical inquiry is bold and also respectful. The preacher honors this inquiry when he or she is vulnerable but not pitiful. The style of preaching should invite both curious questioning and a spiritual experience in the listener.

The third inquiry in liberative narrative preaching is poetic. Poetic inquiry is the least developed of the three. It focuses on the way in which imagination is called forth through encouraging people to uncover their stories and to listen to the many voices speaking from those stories. Metaphor is the primary tool of poetic inquiry. Through metaphor, expressions of narratives can find resonance in people both with and without words.

Liberative narrative preaching populates the landscape of the sermon with metaphors that emerge from the biblical text as well as from the life of the community of faith. An image that a believer remembers from a Bible verse or a religious writing may link with other faith stories that are part of the overall spiritual narrative of the person's life. Further, a community of faith may have metaphors or images of themselves that connect them in meaningful ways to God's story.

Witnessing is perhaps most vividly connected with narratively worshipping. This practice has grown out of favor in most Protestant mainline denominations in favor of an organized, linear style of worship. Some congregations may have separate worship services in which church members have the opportunity to witness about ways God has acted decisively in their lives.

Such witnessing is known as giving testimonies, or testifying. The African American church still has a lively practice of testifying in their worship services. The practice also extends to the celebratory style of preaching (Thomas 1997). Some other congregations that are not African American have discovered that witnessing or testifying has revitalized them. Lillian Daniel recounts the way in which testimonies have drawn congregants together. Long-time members would tell a story that brought new church members into a shared history of the congregation. At the same time, the new church members shared their testimonies of their current church experience, which blended with the stories of the old members (Daniel 2006).

CASE STUDY OF NARRATIVELY WORSHIPPING

A case study of narratively worshipping follows and illustrates some narrative practices. Identifying information has been changed.

Metropolitan Community Hospital partnered with Agape Pastoral Counseling Center to provide a support group for breast cancer survivors. Julie, a staff counselor at Agape Center, volunteered to lead the group. The group represented a variety of denominational backgrounds. However, by chance, all the members were Christians of some persuasion. After a brief time, one of the members requested that they have a brief worship service to express their joys and challenges as they stand up to cancer.

Julie, a pastoral counselor, started the informal worship services. Instead of having Julie preach, the women requested that they share their stories through a time of witnessing. The format became that of reading a passage from the Bible, spending a period of time in silence, and then witnessing to their stories as the Spirit moved them. As the worshipping developed, the members sought to find some connection with other Christian women challenged by cancer.

With the assistance of the hospital, counseling center, and Julie, the women in some major cities offered other support groups for women combating cancer. They then shared their stories with those women through letters, Skype, and videos. The result was mutual support for all the women.

The narrative approach echoed the use of outsider witnessing turned insider witnessing as the women shared their struggle with other women survivors. In addition, the worship experience had some components of a definitional ceremony in which people who successfully battle a problem are recognized in a group setting.

PRACTICES

- To practice narrative leading, engage your congregation, chaplaincy department, or community agency in telling the stories of the group. Divide the group into natural groupings such as study groups or medical floors. Have people write out stories of their engagement when becoming a member of the community. The members then share their stories in increasingly larger groups. Then, repeat the practice by inviting a person to share the spiritual meanings of the group. The final project can be preserved on a DVD that can be updated from year to year in a retreat setting.

- To practice narrative teaching, start an intergenerational Bible study group. Break the group into smaller groups based on age. Invite each age group to determine an image that best represents them. The group then decides what artistic format they will use to represent the image—song, craft, or dance. The groups then share with each other in a worship experience as ritual.

- To practice narrative worshipping, the worship team at your church will formulate a new way to involve church member participation. After a worship service, members will provide feedback on the sermon through story. They will have a period of silence, then share a story about themselves that the sermon evoked. The feedback will continue as stories are shared with others who respond with a theological theme or Bible story that is evoked by the storyteller's story. Finally, the storytellers are challenged to follow the political inquiry of the stories and sermon and share how the stories speak to their own congregation.

5

Storytelling as Spiritual Practice

Spiritual narratives as discussed so far have the capacity to thicken a believer's faith story. That people's personal stories directly affect their faith journey is a foundation for these principles. Stories are understood as a telling of life experience in a form that can be repeated and modified over time. The telling and retelling of the stories as a process itself affords another experience that with the historical events the person is telling both affects and forms his or her identity. As one's identity is changed, different relationships are developed with people. These relationships with people in turn impact the individual person and change that person in some way. Thus, the assumption is that stories are relational.

Relational stories then have a special relationship themselves with Christianity. As Christian faith develops a canon of beliefs and doctrines in addition to a sacred text—the Bible—the assumption is that a vibrant faith is flexible enough to accommodate change. Through changes in the spiritual narrative, people then will be able to engage with their community of faith. The community of faith, in turn, impacts individual believers. And so the mutual formation continues.

This continual forming of spiritual identity through stories of faith can enrich people's lives and their communities of faith. How then would these Christian believers and congregations find a way to make storying and re-storying faith an active, vibrant part of who they are and are becoming? I am proposing storytelling as a spiritual practice. To accomplish this, it will be helpful to first define what a spiritual practice or religious practice actually is.

I will use the term *spiritual practice*. The word *religious* conveys to some people a practice that is connected only with the institutional church. It conveys to others rigidity and inability to change. Given these limitations, I believe that *spiritual practice* conveys a helpful message of flexibility. It is, however, for the purposes of this argument, limited to Christianity.

To connect it with the earlier definition of spirituality, then, spiritual practices refer to how Christians act and reflect on an aspect of their spirituality that is understood to expand them beyond self and relationships to connect with God. Often, Christians may think of a spiritual practice as involving an individual and God, sometimes to the exclusion of a community of faith. However, a connection with a community of faith enriches the spiritual practice for both the individual and community. A community of faith as understood here can be a church but also a group of friends who share similar beliefs.

Storytelling in my view is an overlooked dimension of Christian faith that can be shaped into a spiritual practice. In presenting a map of storytelling as a spiritual practice, several narrative practices will be demonstrated through the creation and collaborative research of a collective narrative methodology called the Staff of Spirit. But first, I will describe the methodology and its development by the Dulwich Centre in Australia.

COLLECTIVE NARRATIVE METHODOLOGY

Over the last few years, Cheryl White and David Denborough of the Dulwich Centre have developed a collective narrative methodology, initially as a response to trauma experience by communities (Madigan 2011). One of the first contexts of this development was Rwanda. Narrative therapists worked with both relief workers and children who were impacted by the genocide. An influential collective narrative methodology called the Tree of Life was developed jointly by Ncazelo Ncube and David Denborough (Denborough 2008).

The Tree of Life was first used with children who were impacted by genocide. The children attended camp that provided a respite for them from the war-drenched environment of their country. But, as soon as they left the camp, they returned back to the trauma they had experienced. The question of what they could take with them that would strengthen their resilience emerged.

The Tree of Life engages the children by lifting up their own strengths and their stories that they share with the whole group. The children draw a tree with roots, ground, trunk, branches, leaves, and fruit. They are instructed to include their heritage and where they are from on the roots; the ground represents their everyday lives; the trunk represents qualities such as generosity and liveliness; branches represent future hopes and dreams; leaves represent important people and pets, both living and dead, as well as toys; flowers represent gifts given by others; and the fruit represent gifts given to others.

Each child shares his or her tree with other children, which is the "telling" of the story. Then, one child summarizes what he or she sees in the tree, which is the "retelling" of the story. Each child is then given a certificate that honors his or her qualities and the ways in which those qualities strengthen the child to stand up to trauma. The certificate is given to them in a *definitional ceremony*. A definitional ceremony in narrative practice is a recognition of a person's knowledges and skills in a community as a ritual.

Collective narrative methodology follows these practices:

> 1. Doubly listening to a story. A story has multiple meanings and doubly listening encourages the listener and storyteller to listen for what is not spoken as well as for underlying storylines. Doubly listening supports listening for an alternate story or counter story that may not be explicit and serves as a counterbalance to the dominant story.
> 2. Engaging both individual and community experiences. A dichotomy between the individual and community thins a story. Weaving both individual and collective telling of stories thickens the story.
> 3. Collective narrative documents. A story is thickened not only by telling a story but also by writing a story. A collective narrative document is created by blending phrases from each individual author into a shared document.
> 4. Songs of sustenance. Writing songs of sustenance follows the practice of collective narrative documents by both creating a melody and writing a lyric that includes phrases written by individual members of a group.
> 5. Story lines that link individuals and communities through the exchanging of messages. Communities who have shared similar loss or trauma but are in different locations write letters of support to each other.

CREATION OF THE STAFF OF SPIRIT

As I began to think about how to connect narrative practice with the enriching of believers' spiritual stories, I reflected on those collective practices I had used, such as the Tree of Life, in different group settings. I was always amazed by how the exercise enriched people's stories on many levels. My dream was to create some instrument that would do the same in a spiritual sense.

I chose a combined symbol of the shepherd's staff and the cross to be used as a visual image that brings forth many resonances for believers of the histories and knowledges of their faith. The cross is the universal symbol for Christianity, and the shepherd's staff has been used to enable believers to remember Christ as the shepherd who cares for the flock. Christians also understand the shepherd's staff as a symbol of compassion and care for others that resonates in other aspects of their spiritual experience. This symbol has the ability, through this resonance, to link the believer to his or her spiritual stories through the narrative development of multileveled stories that in turn can thicken and enrich the believer's faith.

The shepherd's staff is a symbol that has been used in the church for centuries stemming from Psalm 23 in the Hebrew Scriptures, which says, "The Lord is my shepherd," conveying an image of care and protection. The shepherd for the Hebrews looks after the sheep but does not prevent them from wandering around. If the sheep is caught on a rocky ledge, sometimes the shepherd will, in fact, let the sheep stay there for a while so that willfulness wanes and the sheep can be safely scooped up by the crook of the shepherd.

The Staff of Spirit combines the symbol of the staff with the cross, which conveys the image of Jesus Christ who shows his followers ways to stand up to difficulties through compassion and strength and to challenge oppressive beliefs of society. Through his resurrection, Jesus offers liberation to believers from such oppression and an abundant life.

The Staff of Spirit provides a narrative instrument to identify explicit spiritual stories and then, through double-story development, to uncover stories in life and spiritual experience to further deepen believers' faith.[1] Just as a hiker takes a staff to negotiate rocky ledges, so the Staff of Spirit can be used to develop resources for difficult spiritual times.

SPIRITUAL PRACTICE PROCESS

The Staff of Spirit uses storytelling as spiritual practice.[2] It is initially begun through a collective narrative practice that can be conducted as a one day six-hour retreat or as four one-and-a-half-hour sessions over a period of four

1. Hector Hernandez, Christian Theological Seminary graduate, created the Staff of Spirit logo which is included in the appendix for use in this spiritual practice.

2. The Staff of Spirit and other related practices can be accessed on the author's web site, www.spiritualnarratives.com. Pastoral care, ministry, and teaching practices will be shared and updated on a regular basis.

weeks. The target groups would be women's retreats, church groups, spiritual formation groups, and seminary students' pastoral formation groups.

Upon arrival, each participant is given sheets of paper with the Staff of Spirit logo. The facilitator will use a large newsprint pad and a PowerPoint presentation to illustrate the points. When used as four-week sessions, each participant will keep the Staff of Spirit logo sheets as a spiritual journal to keep notes on between the introductory sessions. If the participants are in a one day retreat, then the Staff of Spirit sheets can be used for reflection and note taking during that immediate experience. Extra sheets of the Staff of Spirit are distributed to all participants for use in journaling.

The crook of the Staff of Spirit represents qualities of spirituality for the participant that are connected through relationships with self and others.[3] The cross on the Staff of Spirit represents qualities of spirituality relating to God through Jesus Christ. As participants use the Staff for telling their stories, their present spiritual experiences with significant others and God will be identified. Then, through telling and retelling with other group members functioning as outsider witnesses, the stories will be re-authored and doubly listened to. Stories of sustenance from the past can thus be used as a staff of strength for the future. A believer can choose a different staff for each journey. As a community of faith, we can also share our shepherd's staff with others on the journey. The Staff of Spirit is described as a way to develop storytelling into a spiritual practice that can enrich the participants' faith. Stories can be noted and reflected on in the future. Before beginning the process around the Staff of Spirit, participants are given the primary question the Staff invites: *What sustains you on your journey of faith?*

DESCRIPTION OF GROUPS

Three groups participated in the Staff of Spirit. Group 1 is a group from three rural Presbyterian churches that meet weekly for a Bible study. They agreed to participate in this project and met for four weeks. Group 2 is a group composed of students from Christian Theological Seminary that met for a one-day retreat. Group 3 is another group of students at Christian Theological Seminary that met for four sessions.[4]

3. The Staff of Spirit can be seen in color at www.spiritualnarratives.com. Colors on the Staff have some symbolic imagery from Christian traditions. The lower quadrant is green, representing Jesus as liberator, giver of life, and co-author of story; the upper left quadrant is purple, representing spiritual repentance necessary for new stories; the upper right quadrant is brown, representing place and social location of stories; and the lower right quadrant is red, representing the sustenance of the Spirit.

STAFF OF SPIRIT COLLECTIVE NARRATIVE PROCESS

Participants are given a sheet with the Staff of Spirit logo on it so they can write down their stories and the stories of others, along with significant phrases, for the outsider witness and definitional ceremony at the end of the process. With either silence or quiet music playing, each participant is asked to identify a formative spiritual experience to tell the other members of the group. A *formative spiritual experience* is defined as a spiritual experience that you know is true for you and serves as a source of strength. Taking turns, each participant tells the story of the formative spiritual experience to the group.

SPIRITUAL PRACTICE 1: TELLING YOUR SPIRITUAL STORY

After telling the story, each participant is to write on the crook of the staff, beginning with the lower left quadrant, responses to the following questions:

- *What spiritual qualities does that story call forth in you?* (Lower left quadrant) This question is created to discover the absent but implicit. It is my experience that believers often miss those aspects or "spiritual qualities called forth" of their spiritual stories. It is *implicit* in Christian faith to be meek and modest, not calling attention to those significant qualities that may nurture a spiritual story.
- *What other significant people have a relationship with you through these spiritual qualities?* (Upper left quadrant) This question is created to engage the participant in remembering people who relate with them through these spiritual qualities. Some people may no longer remain in relationship with those qualities while other new people may be admitted to the club of associations. This is also a question where histories of commitments can be explored.
- *What places and contexts do these spiritual qualities take you to?* (Upper right quadrant) This question focuses on the sometimes ignored dimension of place in narrative practice. Recent literature focusing on place can give this question a firmer foundation. Spiritual experience is often focused within a place of worship or meditation. So, remembering can occur here both with people and places.[5]

---

4. Group One met as an informal pilot of the storytelling groups at Old National Road Presbyterian Parish. Groups Two and Three met in accordance with required guidelines of the Institutional Review Board of Christian Theological Seminary.

- *What spiritual qualities draw you closer to God?* (Lower right quadrant) This question reminds participants of God, who can be the ultimate "absent but implicit" even for believers. Many times explicit religious language can miss God, and implicit language and experience can draw God more vividly into the spiritual experience of the believer.

Participants in the four-week group are instructed to reflect daily, during their devotional time, on their story and the responses they have written on the Staff of Spirit. Thoughts, prayers, phrases, biblical stories, and Bible passages that are evoked for them are to be written down and shared at the next meeting. Those who participate in the retreat are to do this practice after the completion of the retreat and then share with a fellow believer.

Spiritual Practice 2: Retelling and Responding

Each participant retells a fellow believer's story of faith and the believer responds to his or her experience of that retelling.

The retelling of the story takes the form of outsider witnesses as each person responds to the story with four questions: What expressions of spirit caught your attention? What images do those spiritual expressions evoke? How do those spiritual expressions resonate with your own experiences? Where do those spiritual experiences transport you?

Some questions to be considered:

- *How has this spiritual story sustained you?* Responding to this question gives the participant an awareness of the effects of the spiritual story and so opens the person to future possibilities for re-storying the whole spiritual narrative.
- *How does this story call for the stories from Scripture?* The absent but implicit here lies in the ability of spiritual stories to reawaken stories from Scripture. In addition, this question invites the believer to notice resonances from other underlying stories.
- *What effects do these stories have on you now?* This question of relative influence can also open possibilities of relationships with the stories and the way in which people and places relating to the spiritual can be remembered.

---

5. Place in narrative practice will be more fully discussed in the next chapter.

- *What does the story call forth in you?* This question evokes the absent but implicit as well as the possibilities for re-authoring the story. Histories of skill and knowledge as well as of relationships may lie fallow but can be reawakened.

Participants serve as outsider witnesses to the story of each person who has shared the story.

SPIRITUAL PRACTICE 3: SPIRITUALITIES OF THE EVERYDAY

Each participant is asked to meditate in silence or with music in the background. The facilitator will say: "You have shared a formative story of faith that has some sacred meaning. As we enter the world each day, we encounter many events and stories that may seem to have no connection with our spiritual story. Think of a challenge of just the past week and reflect on the following questions."

- *What qualities does it call forth from you?* (Write on the crook of the staff.) This is a beginning to re-authoring the dominant spiritual story by connecting the believer to everyday experience in a way similar to Michael White's "exoticizing the common." This explores the challenge of discovering the relationship of seemingly nonspiritual qualities to spiritual qualities that have been explicitly defined.
- *How did it move you to concerns that were bigger than you?* (Write on the cross of the staff.) This moves the believer to a re-storying of those stories both from explicitly spiritual and everyday experiences. The re-storying produces a spiritual narrative of the person's ultimate values and beliefs.
- *Who are you joined with in this challenge?* (Write those names on the staff.) Again, this question evokes re-membering people from the past and present to further enrich the experience of double stories.

Participants share their written responses in the group and the other participants serve as outsider witnesses in the conversation.

SPIRITUAL PRACTICE 4: WITNESSING TO SPIRITUAL STORIES

All participants are asked to select a Staff of Spirit from another participant that would seem to sustain them through life challenges.

- *What stories on the Staff of Spirit most sustain you as you face challenges?* This question evokes the absent but implicit histories of knowledges and relationships that have supported and grown the sustaining stories of faith.
- *What are those challenges?* This question is reminiscent in some ways of Epston's backward story in that the questions in this exercise started on a positive note and now are inviting those challenges through an externalizing question.
- *What qualities do you need for this challenge?* Through the question, the believer is drawn to a deeper level of double story in reflecting on what qualities are needed for this everyday challenge. He or she can reflect on ways in which those qualities call forth histories of knowledges and relationships that can be woven in the re-authored story.

As a definitional ceremony, the participant groups are asked to select one of the following options: (1) The group can create a banner to be hung in the sanctuary. Each person is asked to create a small square with an image on it that symbolizes the story that sustains them now. (2) The group can write a song that can be sung in a worship service. (3) The group can write a litany that blends some phrase each person's story retelling which can be used in a worship service.

SUMMARIES OF STAFF OF SPIRIT EXPERIENCES

Three groups participated in the Staff of Spirit storytelling groups. Different methodologies were employed to identify what spiritual practice process was most effective. The first group served as a pilot to refine the process. Then, groups two and three were given a pre-test and post-test which asked the participants to evaluate their ability to connect their personal stories with their spiritual growth. Group three's post-test showed that after their Staff of Spirit group, they were better able to make a connection between their personal stories and spiritual growth. Group two expressed little growth in finding stronger spiritual connections with life stories after their one day experience.

GROUP 1

This group met for four weeks in lieu of a Bible study they usually had. I used this group to pilot test the Staff of Spirit process and determine how to tweak it. We followed the process listed over the four weeks. Initially, I assigned each person only one other person to listen to their story. This approach was not effective because sometimes people missed the next session where the storytelling occurred. (In future groups, I had the retelling of the retelling take place in an outsider witness setting with all persons participating.) The group identified the following phrases as important from the participants' stories: "Jesus, you are my shelter in a time of storm." "God will take care of you." "Jesus, you are the light." The phrases were woven into a prayer that was used in worship at each of the churches.

GROUP 2

Group 2 met for a one-day retreat using the spiritual practice process described above. After the process was finished, the outsider witnesses lifted up phrases from the stories that were powerful and also held meaning for the storyteller. Heather told about God talking with her in the words, "I will give you courage in time of trial." May, who saw Jesus in her apartment, said he said to her, "Follow me with obedience and courage." Jane heard Jesus speak to her, "I will be with you always. I will hold you." They wrote the following prayer (words of the storytellers are italicized) and then closed with a definitional ceremony as they joined hands and prayed the prayer.

> Holy God, we praise you for sustaining and guiding us through life's challenges, for *giving us courage in time of trial*. Help us to remain open to your voice and to know that your presence is *with us always*. When we are unsure of the road to take, may it be your path we *follow with obedience and courage*. Help us to claim your promises to us in order that we may be purified and made whole in you. Teach us to show your love and compassion to everyone around us so that you may be seen through us. For we can do all things through Christ who strengthens us. Amen.

GROUP 3

Group 3 was composed of four women who met over a period of four weeks using the spiritual practice process described above. One spiritual practice took place each week. A palpable sense of connection between the women occurred over the period of time. Tawny told a story in which a friend introduced her to a person at a bar. Quite unexpectedly, they got into a conversation about her search for God. His last words to her were, "Don't let Satan steal from you what God has given." This happened over a round of Little Kings—a brand of beer in the United States. Sherri told of her connection with her grandmother, who told many Bible stories to her. She always held to the story of Hagar, who was left in the wilderness and for whom God provided. She said, "Through these stories, my faith has become my own." Laurie told of her searching until she found the right church. For years, she felt guilty about leaving her former church. She closed by saying, "I just kept moving until I found the right place." The following description focuses primarily on Sally while also indicating the group process that occurred through the four-week period in order to give a more detailed view of the process.

SALLY'S STORY

Sally is a member of Group 3. She joined the storytelling group because of her interest in stories and spiritual direction. Sally underwent breast cancer surgery over a year ago and has had chemotherapy for months, which has stabilized the progression of the cancer. A chaplain, she is an ordained minister in a Protestant denomination. As the group began, all the participants shared why they joined the group. In addition to her interests, Sally said, "I love to weave tapestries, and when I sit at the wheel, I think of the tapestries as having a story. It's much like the stories I hear from patients, and now, I'm a patient."

Each member of the group shared their interest in the storytelling group: Sherri said she loved narrative therapy, Laurie said she was intrigued by stories, and Tawny said that she used stories in her church. After these brief introductions, each person was invited to go somewhere quiet in the building and for fifteen to twenty minutes to reflect on and find a "formative spiritual experience" to share with the rest of the group.

When the group members returned, everyone told their story. Soon, it was Sally's turn and she told the following story:

I had a visitation one night. I've always been very rational about my faith. And being a liberal church minister, I never paid much attention to unexplained things. One night I was lying in bed with so much pain. I had tried everything. I tried to clear my mind. And I'm just lying there. And then I felt Jesus' presence. I didn't see anything. But, I felt him. I hadn't asked for anything. But, the pain left. I was able to sleep. I've never tried to explain it. It was not rational which is how I process faith. I can't explain it. It wasn't so much what I believed as what I needed.

After Sally told her story, I asked each participant to take the Staff of Spirit sheets. Following the description of the process described above, each person was asked to write on the Staff the answers to those questions. Sally answers were as follows: *What spiritual qualities does that story call forth in you?* Learning and persevering. *What other significant people have a relationship with you through these spiritual qualities?* My husband, daughter, and all the women at the cancer treatment center. *What places and contexts do these spiritual qualities take you to?* They take me to my loom and weaving. *What spiritual qualities draw you closer to God?* I don't ask for healing from the cancer but look at cancer as a teacher.

The participants were asked to take the Staff of Spirit sheet with their notes on it home with them. They were asked to reflect daily on their story and their written responses.

The next week began with people responding to the stories of the previous week. The group members functioned as outsider witnesses responding to the participants' stories. When it was time for Sally's story, the following conversation occurred:

Sherri: I was so moved by your story, Sally. That phrase. . . [looks at notes] "It wasn't so much what I believed as what I needed." I marvel at how you can say that with cancer.

Sally: I look to cancer as my teacher. The visitation was what I needed. That's what gets me from day to day.

Sherri: Sally, your story reminds me of my story. I never felt like I was strong or able. And last week, as I thought of my grandmother's telling me Bible stories, I realized that the story for me was Hagar—she [was] left in the wilderness. You were left in the wilderness. And then you had that visitation. . . .

Sally: Yes, yes, I'm not in the wilderness anymore. I received what I needed just like your Hagar. I can see my story in your story.

Before the session ended, the participants considered the following questions and were asked to reflect on them during the coming week in their journaling: *How has this spiritual story sustained you? How does this story call for the stories from Scripture? What effects do these stories have on you now? What does the story call forth in you?*

The third week began with asking the participants to reflect on a challenge they had during the past week and then to reflect in silence on the following questions, writing their answers on the Staff of Spirit: *What qualities does the challenge call forth from you? How did it move you to concerns that were bigger than you? Who are you joined with in this challenge?*

After the participants wrote their answers down on the Staff, they shared their responses with the group. Sally shared her challenge of the past week. She spoke,

Sally: I had some tests run. And I had been cancer free. But, the cancer has recurred. I have to have radiation.
[The group was silent, and then Sherri spoke.]
Sherri: I'm so sorry, Sally. Is there something we can do for you?
Sally: Just being here is important. I wrote down on my Staff that I am joined with all of you. Your stories have somehow become my story. Especially your story of Hagar—being out there in the wilderness.

The other women spoke, responding to Sally, listening in depth as outsider witnesses.

The fourth week began as participants were asked to select another person's Staff of Spirit for the journey of faith. Not surprisingly, Sally and Sherri chose each other's staffs. They were then asked the following questions: What stories on the Staff of Spirit most sustain you as you face challenges? What are those challenges? What qualities do you need for this challenge?

Sally: [Laughing] Of course, I'd like to take on Sherri's Hagar. Can I?
Sherri: Of course you can. And your visitation I'd like to have.

Sally: Of course.

The other women responded with laughter and tears.

The conversation as outsider witnesses was rich, so we decided to add an extra session so that the group could create an artistic document and have a definitional ceremony to end their time together. The group decided that they would make a banner with the image of each woman's story that the outsider witnesses had lifted up.

For Tawny, the image was a crown to commemorate the Little Kings. Sherri's image was a fountain with water to remember God providing for Hagar in the wilderness. Laurie's image was a heart with a cross to mark her finding a space of worship that was right in her heart. And for Sally, the image was a pitcher to represent healing oil for her journey.

After the banner was made, a definitional ceremony of acknowledgments was held to say good-bye with the presentation of a hat Sherri had knit for Sally as a gift from the group. The group did not want good-bye. The group planned to meet regularly and to invite others in the seminary community to join them.

POSSIBILITIES FOR THE STAFF OF SPIRIT

The Staff of Spirit is used here in a collective narrative sense. And as the familiarity with the Staff grew, I have become aware that each of the spiritual exercises itself could be used as a separate process, but one that interconnects with the others. The first exercise could be applicable for narrative therapy with a therapist who has Christian clients. By using the Staff, the therapist would not need to be Christian but could respect the client's beliefs by using the Staff as an instrument to deepen faith.

The first three spiritual practices could be used for individual meditation by omitting the outsider witnessing. At a later time, perhaps, the believer could invite friends of faith to become outsider witnesses. Thus, there would be the possibility for both individual and community response.

Finally, I can see how persons of different faiths could select a symbol of their faith, for example, the moon and crescent for Muslims or the Star of David for Jews, to focus on for their spiritual story. Possibilities for the absent but implicit of these faiths would exist as other stories of faith resonate with their believers.

Future study groups focusing on the Staff of Spirit will begin. Hopefully, new possibilities for its use as an instrument of rich spiritual story development can grow. The Staff will serve as a support through the challenges of faith's journey.

Spiritual Formation for Individuals

The Staff of Spirit is a spiritual practice involving group process. Another narrative spiritual practice for individuals is described in my book *Re-storying Your Faith.* Detailed questions and a process guide can be found in that book. The spiritual process invites believers to allow a spiritual experience that can be storied to come to mind. First, the individual is asked to "discover your formative spiritual experience." Then, the experiences are recorded in some fashion. Lift up the themes in each experience. Then, identify which experience you want to story to yourself. Write or record your story.

The second step is to "tell your spiritual story." Identify what fruits of the spirit are linked to this story. Reflect upon the effect of those spiritual gifts upon your life.

Third, "reflect on your spiritual story." You now reflect upon how the spiritual story sustains you. Go further and identify connections between your story and any biblical stories.

Fourth, "respond to your spiritual story." Think about ways in which these spiritual gifts may help address any challenges in your life. Then, go further by reflecting about the connections between these spiritual resources and the everyday stories. These everyday stories may be easy to overlook. By taking a step back and reflecting, one's spiritual resiliency can be deepened (Coyle 2013).

Engaging in this personal spiritual practice can be used in different ways in collaboration with the Staff of Spirit. One can use the personal spiritual practice before participating in the Staff of Spirit. It can also be used as a follow-up to the spiritual group process. Of course, it can be used without the Staff of Spirit.

Both spiritual practices can be used either as one time or ongoing experiences. They lend themselves to used during Advent or Lent. True to narrative practice, there is not just one story to re-story. Participants can keep records of the spiritual stories that are storied and then make connections with other stories. In this way, spiritual narratives are uncovered and richly thickened to aid in faith development.

Practices

- Find a church group or group of friends to experience the Staff of Spirit. This spiritual practice can be used for a lay leader's retreat, a pastors support group, or a seminary students retreat.
- Begin your own personal spiritual practice. Using *Re-storying Your Faith* or another spiritual guide of your choice, you begin your spiritual journey. Share those experiences with another believer.

6

Spiritual Narratives of Place

Uncovering stories of our lives that richly develop our spirituality so far has focused on those stories that live within our memories of the past and our hopes for the future. These stories are often populated by those relationships, values, and hopes that give meaning to our lives. Re-storying or re-authoring asks us to consider the effects of these stories on the people in our lives as well as on our hopes and dreams. The inhabitants of these stories are largely the significant people in our lives who deepen our spirituality and connect us more closely to God.

Place unwittingly may be left out of this deepening of our spiritual stories. It is easy to view location or place as merely the site where the stories are told. Stories occur somewhere. True, it is relating to people that our life is truly infused with meaning. Therefore, we may leave the place where the meaning of relationships occurred behind us.

Place, however, has a rich history in lives of believers. The Hebrews' spiritual identity developed from a wandering people worshipping a traveling God to a people with a transportable ark as place to worship God. Then, the temple at Jerusalem was built where the ark rested. The Hebrews found a place of spiritual focus—Jerusalem—to enrich their worship of God.

Similar experiences may occur in our own lives. We remember the church where we made a profession of faith. The mountain trail where we experienced God's presence is a place we may visit whenever possible. The church where a couple was married may remind them of the first love they experienced. As we revisit the places where deep spiritual experiences occurred, we might experience the story related to that place in a new way. Our spiritual story is deepened.

This chapter explores the role of place in spiritual narratives as informed by narrative practice, liberation theology, and the rich collaboration between them. After discussing these discrete features, I will explicate a narrative pedagogy through the experience of students and professor in a cultural immersion class of Christian Theological Seminary through Appalachian Ministries Educational Resource Center (AMERC) that took place in the Appalachian region of eastern Kentucky. Finally, I will draw implications for pastors and seminary professors from the research findings of the class, lifting "place" as an important component of contextual ministry with a unique emphasis on social justice for marginalized populations.

PLACE IN NARRATIVE PRACTICE

As one considers place, a review of the narrative practice literature reveals little that is explicitly connected with place. Australian native Jane Lester (2001) and the New Zealand Just Therapy Team (Raheimet al. 2004) offer reflections on ways in which land is linked to identity through narrative therapy. The richest description of place in narrative therapy comes from an article by Mark Trudinger (2006) in which he reviews its role and offers some suggestions for further development through reflection on his leading a workshop with young men suffering the effects of violence.

The practice of narrative therapy, however, has several implicit references to place. Michael White's questions for reflecting teams focus on expressions, image, resonance, and transport (2007). The last category of transport asks, "Where does it 'transport' you to?" This question implies that different experiences inhabit different places—those spheres to which we may find ourselves "transported" so that literally we are in a different "space." Further, White's last contribution to narrative therapy was the idea of "maps" of narrative practice as a metaphor of how to find one's way through the landscapes of action and identity (2007). However, the relationship of place itself to identity in narrative therapy has not been richly explored (Trudinger 2006).

In Trudinger's deepening of anthropologist Barbara Myerhoff's writing about an elderly Jewish community in Santa Monica, he argues that people do not merely inhabit space, but "inscribe themselves on it" (Trudinger 2006, 12). These inscriptions are ways in which people interpret and reflect on themselves based on the environment in which they live. This engagement with space can be seen as "the physical" (walls), "spatial and cultural" (neighborhoods), and more mobile and less place-bound aspects of culture (media) (12).

This introduces the notion of space as a dimension of human experience. How do we inhabit our physical space? To what degree do we experience the physicality of life? Where do connections with our communities and neighborhoods enrich or deplete our identities? These questions come to my mind in thinking about the relationship we as humans have with our physical spaces. Communities and neighborhoods develop specific reputations and identifiers. Often, inner-city communities carry the weight of a negative connotation where suburban communities carry the imprint of all good. News commentators may express little surprise at a perpetrator of crime who hails from the inner city but have shocked expressions when the same perpetrator is a suburban resident.

Place and physical space have the potential to link with the dominant cultural discourse that is at the heart of narrative practice. Narrative therapy understands people's problem saturated stories to be caused by the cultural discourses or by conversations that are accepted as the norm. As discussed so far, many dominant cultural discourses do not fit with what a person may prefer as his or her identity. As narrative practitioners then encourage the less-explored stories, those stories contribute to the person's identity largely through the dimension of time. Developing one's identity through stories, then, becomes a way for the re-storying to consider the past, present, and future tenses of story. However, time in people's lives is always contained in space and place. The event happens somewhere.

Drawing from this observation, space has always been a part of human history while at the same time little discussed in the exploration of people's identities. This is especially seen in psychotherapy as the therapist expands a person's story largely through relationships and sense of self over a period of time. The "places" of a person's life are largely seen as benchmarks for the events of time.

Time and the passage of time are honored in Western thought. As Trudinger discusses, this privileging of time over space has some real implications for considerations of power. Foucault's (2006) treatment of power, which is used as a foundational concept of narrative therapy, has the capacity to address both time and space, particularly through the common use of metaphor. It is essential to consider space in understanding people's lives. "Space is fundamental in any form of communal life; space is fundamental in any exercise of power" (Foucault 1984, 252).

Trudinger identifies some understandings that emerge from questions about space: (1) physical spaces in which we live are the products of culture and history; (2) identity is formed in the context of these spaces; (3) while some spaces such as schools, prisons, and so on affect what is formed within them, there are always resistances; and (4) meanings of space are contested through the connection with these places (2006).

In addition to these identified understandings, marginalized groups such as women and persons of color experience clear effects of places and space on their identities. Feminists have inquired into the differences of spaces and places. Spaces that are determined to be public during the day become men's places at night (Fairfax 2005). Such public spaces that are safe during the day become dangerous at night and women are excluded. Feminists also respond to the ways in which the planning of public building such as schools and workplaces does not allow for a feminist engagement or sensibility, instead engendering a largely masculine ethos of space. Ecofeminists lift up concerns of the place of ecology in feminist thinking as well as the role of feminist thinking in ecology. The impact of economics and production on women and children as well as conversations about third world development are also related to feminist concerns about place (Trudinger 2006).

These feminist arguments from Euro-feminists would certainly be countered by womanist theologians in the United States who would argue that white feminists still have the advantage of white privilege regardless of the ethos of the space. This provides a bridge to concerns by persons of color who, in addition to the concerns of white feminists, would join with womanists lifting up extreme disruptions of place through colonization and slavery. The effects of colonization have impacted not only the lives of humans themselves but also the native flora and fauna of living areas.

Further, industrialized countries have experienced a profound loss of connection of human life to the land, and this looms on the horizon for indigenous people such as the natives of the Brazilian rainforest and the aboriginals of Australia. Long ago the Native Americans of the United States lost most of their land and have been relegated to live on reservations. Demographic studies of Native Americans can make the argument for the demise of their placed ethnic and religious identity has contributed to the high rate of alcoholism and suicide in extant Indian tribes.

It would seem that such considerations of space or place would find resonance in narrative therapy. Certainly, liberation theology offers grounding in place as it champions marginalized persons who do not have access to the socioeconomic advantage often closely connected with a place. Freire's pedagogy that advocates flipping the structure to engage with the oppressed is influenced by the abject conditions of place that adversely impact persons living in squalid living spaces.

Some liberation theologies may support the idea that place has an ultimate effect on humans. At the same time, an assumption is that humans can adjust to various spaces. An alternative that Trudinger draws is "to read and listen to people's diverse and particular accounts of how they engage with place, and how they regard this engagement" (2006, 16).

Trudinger offers some questions from a narrative perspective: "How do individuals and communities relate to the places they live in? How does the relationship of people to places change over time? How might place be constitutive of identity? What effects might places have on relations of class, gender, sexuality, and age? How does the negotiation of identity in place alter both places and identities?" (Trudinger 2006, 16). In addition to these specific questions, just reflecting upon place—"current places, lost places, special places, imaginary places, 'difficult' places, everyday places, and even places that are the location of dreams about the future" (16)—can have a lasting effect on persons.

Imagination about living in future places can offer scaffolding for undeveloped spiritual narratives. Developing one's imagination can find a place through metaphor as we envision different living in different spaces where our preferred spiritual narrative can be developed. This link of imagination and place connects with the developing method of inquiry through poetics (Epston 2013). Imagination further connects with the potential of a person's experiencing liberation from present oppressive experiences and places.

Liberation theology has elements that have not been broadly developed past its close connection with socioeconomic justice. One of these is the theology of hope as explicated in current liberation theology with the emphasis on hope for the future as being experienced in the present. This, as previously discussed, does fit well with narrative practice. Hope through the lens of liberation theology, I believe, can develop Trudinger's notion of "location of dreams about the future."

Biblical writers often lifted up place as an important route to hope, such as the Promised Land. Abraham and Sarah's faithfulness was tested as God instructed them to move to a new place, leaving their land holdings. Jesus' mission to the world was inaugurated through baptism at the River Jordan. His gift of life to us was given on a cross at Calvary. These places and others in Scripture were more than places. They served as contexts where spiritual narratives of believers were deepened. Rich memories of those places expanded the believers' identities.

Quite naturally, reflections on significant places lead to broader thoughts about the environment and its context (Trudinger 2006). People who have spiritual experiences in places blessed by a beautiful vision may take that vision to enrich their faith through visual memories. In contrast, people who live their lives in squalid conditions do not have the luxury of placing their experiences in a beautiful context that can enrich them.

This reflection does raise the question of whether an oppressive context prohibits an experience that has enriching capacities for one's spiritual narrative. The answer seems to be "no" when one reflects in particular on the experience of people who, living in slavery, develop rich lives of faith as illustrated by the Hebrew people in the Bible and African Americans in our country's history. Intrinsic to these experiences is a vision of an environment that is beautiful and welcome—the golden streets of heaven, not the dank hull of a slave ship. The music of spirituals that transport the believers to a different place is born in such contexts.

The context of liberation theology offers narrative practice's exploration of place a rich journey to take. Liberation theology originated in contexts of South American poverty where the primary purpose was to lift up people oppressed by such conditions. Liberation theology thus began with the concern of socioeconomic conditions connected with place. Yet, it did not stop there. It expanded to concerns of African Americans in black theology, feminists, and womanists.

Liberation theology has been criticized for being tethered to socioeconomic conditions and the spirit of this world. Yet, it does not remain there. Hope in the future is a critical component of liberation theology. It seeks to lift up future "hopes and dreams," as narrative would describe it, so that people can envision and dream of a future where dominant discourses are lifted. While looking to the future, liberation theology believes that it is critical to change living conditions—the place of the present—so that people can have physical relief and breathe in spiritual hope. Thus, as humans we are inextricably joined with the physical, the concreteness of place.

Looking to the spaces of this world and envisioning hopes and dreams of liberation remain grounded together in liberation theology. The liberative focus on the current political ethos of people's spaces links well with narrative inquiry, which focuses on political inquiry. Narrative political inquiry takes place through collective narrative practice that transports the telling and retelling of stories to other geographical communities where the stories' resonances with similar experiences there thicken spiritual narratives. Thus, both narrative practice and liberation theology share a focus on expanding our stories so others may be empowered.

This sensibility of liberation theology offers richness for further narrative questioning of place. The lifting up of hope in liberation has already set several metaphors that contribute to thickening spiritual narratives. "The realm or kingdom of God," "with the community of saints," and "the throne of God" are all metaphorical places that at the same time connect with an exploration of spiritual identities. Place and person become connected. These phrases used in other theologies gain a special depth in liberation theology through the focus on both present and future.

Narrative practices that are more focused on place require that pastoral caregivers concentrate on inquiries that thicken such awareness. Trudinger offers orienting questions: How can we listen to implicit or explicit references to spaces and places? What might happen if we ask about people's relationship with places over time? How might people prefer to relate to the spaces in their lives? What places do people find that help them be more in touch with preferred accounts of their lives? What importance might considerations of place take when arranging rituals? How might physically changing the place in itself be a rite of passage? (Trudinger 2006, 16–17).

Liberation theology, at this point, offers narrative practice a particularly fertile ground to grow spiritual narratives. The "what" of liberation theology does not yield to the "how" and "where" of liberation theology. Theologians who espouse a liberative framework acknowledge the content of faith while always understanding it in the context of place and process. Liberative theological themes can richly thicken the "why" of narrative practice when it points to a God who lifts up the oppressed.

This process of liberation theology can thicken narrative's emphasis of storying lives in terms of identity and relationships. A hermeneutical circle of context, reflection, and action with a continual position of prayer describes a process of liberating persons so that they have the capacity for rich spiritual narratives that are, in turn, used to invite others to experience liberation as well. Such a process has some similarity to narrative re-storying and practices of outsider witnesses. It also has the potential to link to collective narrative practice in a methodology that honors place and person. Such was my and several seminary students' experiences as we participated in a cultural immersion course informed by liberative narrative practices. We turn to that discussion prefaced by an understanding of methodology that can be used in such cultural immersion courses.

Contributions to a Liberative Narrative Pedagogy

Narrative practice historically has never done much research to validate its approaches empirically. Its interest has focused on exploring the rich land of stories through honoring a person's expertise on his or her own landscape of narratives. At the same time, actual narrative practice in the therapy room has repeatedly been referred to as "co-research" because of its emphasis on the therapist engaging in the re-storying or re-authoring of people's stories as an influential editor of narratives (Epston and White 1992).

Compatible methodologies of pastoral practice can lend themselves to thickened explorations of place as context for spiritual narratives. Current practice of pastoral research focuses largely on ethnography understood as "a way of immersing yourself in the life of a people in order to learn something about and from them"(Moschella 2008, 4). Moschella's research methodology understands itself to draw from narrative models of theology and care due to its recognition of storytelling as a hallmark of human experience.

A related method is Savage and Presnell's narrative approach, which focuses on learning from the story by first uncovering the narratives then externalizing the story. The process moves to deconstructing the story by separating the narrative of concern from the preferred story of the storyteller. The last step is rewriting the story, which moves from transformation to starting over with uncovering the narratives. This story process contextualizes in the understanding of who God is in the life of the believer (Savage and Presell 2008).

These approaches, while intended for formal research studies, contribute to narrative pedagogical techniques. Weaving through both research methods are a respect for story, a recognition of the impact of the "co-researcher" on participants, and engagement of the co-researcher in the participant's community.

These approaches resonate with current themes of collective narrative practice, which to review, are as follows: (1) As we listen to stories of individuals and groups, we conceive of them as representing both personal experience as well as the effects of broader social issues. (2) Individuals, groups, and communities respond to the situations they are in. (3) We do not bring our own initiatives but uncover the hopes and dreams that are implicit in people's responses. (4) Once local skills and values are documented, we seek an audience with whom these will resonate. (5) Those persons in the community are encouraged to make a contribution of their experience to others. (6) Intergenerational contributions are always encouraged. (7) People's responses to hardship are forms of local social action that may be linked with other actions. (8) Generation and performance of "local folk culture" such as written word, spoken word, song, film, dance poetry, and celebration can be shared within definitional ceremonies that contribute to rich identity. (9) Friere's "invention of unity in diversity" is honored. And (10) we need to approach this work with a broad view and future contribution as Freire envisioned (Denborough 2008).

These themes of collective narrative practice were previously considered in the research project that culminated in the Staff of Spirit. Some of the concerns that led to that project originated in the first cultural immersion course I taught in Appalachia. In that first pedagogical context, I pondered about a method and process that would be consistent with a narrative approach. As I participated in the International Training Program in Narrative Therapy and Community Work at the Dulwich Centre, I came to appreciate the care with which the pedagogical context was set.

Cheryl White, for instance, uses the phrase "widening the focus of the round" to refer to intentionally focusing on what persons with whom we work might want us to accomplish during training (2008, 35). The Dulwich faculty, at the beginning of the training, ask the trainees what hopes their "clients" might have for them in this endeavor. The further concern is to check in with their "clients" periodically during the training. Such pedagogy encourages a thickening of the telling process of the learning experience.

Narrative pedagogy is always focused on the experience of the participants, how that experience impacts them, and ways in which the entire learning community is impacted. All participants engage in a thickening of story through telling, retelling, and retelling the retelling. The experience of participating in the storytelling process enriches the stories of individuals and their communities as those stories are shared.

However, the stories and their contribution to individual identity are not all that is enriching. Place is an enriching context that often is not part of the teaching experience except for a brief line on evaluations asking about the comfortableness of the meeting place. Place offers a richness to story that encourages a person's rootedness in his or her identity. In particular, a teaching context also provides space that offers engagement with individuals and community in the integration of ideas and lived experience. Cultural immersion classes offer an ideal environment for such growth. They are generally thought of as part of a seminary curriculum. However, after a description of the present Appalachian cultural immersion class, implications will be drawn for using a cross-cultural experience in a congregational setting to expand the social justice awareness of congregants.[1]

---

1. I am currently consulting with Rev. Jeffrey Bower and the congregation of St. John's Episcopal Church in Speedway, Indiana as they prepare for their Appalachian Pilgrimage in summer 2014. Publication about this congregational cultural experience is planned.

Liberative Narrative Approaches to Cultural Immersion Experiences

I never dreamed of creating a cultural immersion course in Appalachia to add to my pedagogical repertoire. Yet, several storylines in my life formed spiritual narratives that I began to uncover as my teaching career developed. As I tell my experience, I will illustrate the stories that connect to this chapter's foundation of looking at place as critical ground for thickening one's spiritual identity.

I never took much notice of eastern Kentucky or Appalachia when I was a child growing up on a farm in central Kentucky. Eastern Kentucky was viewed as being different from us—as a place where roads were bad and education poor. My father hailed from the central part of the state, but my mother was proudly raised behind a creek in the knob land bordering the mountains of eastern Kentucky.

Education, however, was our family value, and its narrative impacted our lives. My father, who farmed without college education yet with an intelligent wit, supported a total of six college and graduate degrees between my mother, who was a teacher, and me, an avid student. So, when I moved to Princeton, New Jersey, to attend Princeton Theological Seminary, I did not expect to become more deeply connected with my land heritage in the knobs and eastern Kentucky.

It began with an innocent visit to purchase an item at a store within two weeks of arriving in New Jersey. I asked the sales clerk, "Do you have a sack for this?" She looked rather quizzically at me, replying, "Ma'am, we don't have sacks—only bags." This exchange confirmed that I was in a foreign land. Not even the common language of "sack" was recognized here. Next came having my accent worked on in speech lab, only to be capped by random comments wondering aloud about Kentucky and implying that I must be one of the few intelligent people in the state.

I found myself identifying more and more with the hills of eastern Kentucky. Despite the careful delineation that central Kentucky was not eastern Kentucky, these foreigners identified the whole state of Kentucky as having the same culture as eastern Kentucky. While distinct regional differences do exist in the state, I found the rebel in me claiming my mother's knob land heritage and understanding myself in a different light as an adopted "hillbilly."

After I returned to my native homeland, I provided pastoral counseling in eastern Kentucky for years before moving to Indianapolis. As I began my career at Christian Theological Seminary, I became involved with Appalachian Ministries Educational Resource Center (AMERC) as a member of the board of directors. Quite serendipitously, I became interested in narrative therapy and in offering a cultural immersion course in eastern Kentucky through AMERC.

In designing the first cultural immersion course taught in eastern Kentucky through AMERC, I wanted to integrate narrative therapy with liberation theology through mountain stories. The notion of place from my own experience in my move to New Jersey figured largely in the creation of the course. Both courses varied in some degree. However, several components were similar in both courses: indigenous mountain stories representing folk psychology as well as being expressions of art, an identification of dominant cultural discourse, a communal living situation, engagement with local people, immersion in folk art forms, and reflection on narrative practice and liberation theology. For the purposes of this discussion, only the most recent Appalachian cultural immersion class will be reviewed.

The participants were students from several seminaries who were fulfilling their cultural immersion degree requirement. The course began in a retreat setting where the students and teacher began to get to know each other through a collective narrative practice, the Tree of Life. In the Tree of Life, persons draw a tree and trace the histories, skills, and knowledges that contribute to their identity. The components are roots—where you come from and your heritage; ground—everyday life; trunk—skills and knowledges; branches—hopes and dreams; leaves—significant persons in your life; fruit—your gifts to others; and fruit—growth to others (Denborough 2008).

Participants tell their story as depicted on the tree, then another person tells the presenter's story as he or she sees it. Next, all the trees are placed on the wall so that the participants can see the strengths of the community of trees. This process introduces the beginning narratives of each person and thickens their relationships as they tell each other's stories (Denborough 2014).

To develop their spiritual narratives, the participants went through the Staff of Spirit spiritual formation process, which is described in an earlier chapter. The telling of their personal histories and lineage, along with their spiritual narratives, resulted in a thickening of spiritual narratives. This spiritual retreat provided a context for students to take on the de-centered and influential stance of the storyteller of hope.

Prior to the retreat, participants were asked to read native mountain stories from such regional authors as Jesse Stuart, George Ella Lyon, and James Still. Themes from these books were highlighted to understand further values, hopes, and dreams of the people. Intrinsic to these stories was the folk psychology of the regional people—appreciation for the land, independence, perseverance, love of family, and rootedness to the land. These cultural discourses are, of course, a part of the region's identity. At the same time, dominant cultural discourse about Appalachia includes the idea that its inhabitants are uneducated and lazy (Coyle 2011).

The class looked at the dominant cultural discourses that impacted the area as well as how place and environment connected with the narratives of people's lives. Embedded in this narrative was the impact of coal mining as an income source, along with the impact of coal mining on the region. Dominant discourses clashed at this point. A significant portion of the cultural experience focused on dialogue with native Appalachians to learn respect for the culture and just sit with the people.[2]

We then reflected on ways in which these dominant cultural discourses have oppressed the people of eastern Kentucky. Liberation theology was brought into conversation as the mountain stories in the written word and the oral stories were told and retold. The liberative process of De La Torre is tied to the hermeneutical method of liberation theology through the following process: observing the social situation, reflecting narratively and theologically upon the situation and its geographical place, praying, and determining the action. Opportunities for social activism in the mountains were also discussed along with opportunities to connect with communities with similar challenges so that all may be strengthened.

RESPONSES OF CLASS PARTICIPANTS

Class participants expressed a variety of reactions to the cultural immersion experience. Some had a difficult time understanding the unique challenges that Appalachians face before the experience. A female student puzzled, "How is living here any different? If people work hard they can change their lives."

As the days grew into weeks, attitudes softened. One student said, "I thought it was just silly for people here to be so sensitive and untrusting of outsiders. But, now I understand their initial hesitancy. There's so much here that's rich that's just ignored."

Slowly, the complexity of being valued on where you live dawned upon the students' awareness. At first, students thought that anyone who went into Appalachia had the right to tell the story. Toward the end of the class, the question "Who has the story-telling rights?" impacted us all. Our answer

---

2. The narrative practitioners at the Dulwich Centre consult with communities around the globe. Prior to a consultation, they spend time with the local people to begin to break down barriers of misunderstanding and prejudice.

became "the person whose story it is" (Narrative Charter, www.dulwichcentre.com.au, accessed 2013).

Implications for Contextual Ministry and Social Justice

The cultural immersion class "Mountain Stories: Re-storying Spiritual Narratives", described in the syllabus of the resources section (in the appendix), offers some possibilities for liberative narrative practices in teaching and congregational contexts. An initial step is to determine the place to which the seminary or congregation has the strongest connection. Contextual ministry can focus on a local place or some place that is regional or international in scope. The narrative criterion is that the "place" offers the potential of connecting with the stories of the participants to offer them a thickened spiritual narrative.

Participants then need to engage in some kind of spiritual retreat where a context of community for individual stories can be experienced with some attention to how those stories thicken each other. This process needs to honor the telling, retelling, and retelling of the retelling in community. This recognizes the telling of individual stories, a witness telling that person's story, and the community responding to the storytelling process.

Contextual ministry and education then participates in collective narrative practice by honoring folk culture through expressions of writing, art, music, and dance. Possibilities include an art project for a seminary class, a banner for a church, or a musical composition that represents a visual image, spoken expression, or written word that brings forth the themes of the narratives of the person.

Visiting or living at the place of spiritual connection highlights the need for lived experience. It further reflects on ways in which the place and connection with that space can bring forth memories of the past that richly connect with the present. It further thickens one's identity.

A ritual to honor contextual ministry or education further thickens the storytelling. Student presentations that involve the entire class are one example for a class. A worship service that integrates some of the folk art, such a litany, prayer, or song, could be enriching for a congregation.

Connection with a broader community that has experienced a similar place or context not only lessens a feeling of isolation and oppression but also offers a possibility of living out liberation theology by changing the lives of people from the bottom up. As people experience places through storytelling stories that did not exist or that they did not remember, hopes and dreams will emerge. Mucherera presents the possibility of using a particular space to interact with hope for the future through his narrative pastoral counseling in a postcolonial context. As he explores the *palaver*, a meeting place for Africans to resolve personal and social problems, he challenges us to get out of our counseling rooms (Mucherera 2009). Perhaps we can find such places on the picket lines, in lobbying groups, or at the soup kitchen.

Social justice then becomes possible as people's spiritual lives are enriched. Through such growth, people pay more attention to social location and our embodied experience (Townsend, 2009). Changes for people who feel oppressed then can come through the lived experience of Freire's maxim of "unity through diversity" in contextual ministry.

PRACTICES

- All persons have some experiences of marginalization (race, culture, gender, sexual orientation and so on). Think about an experience when you felt marginalized. Talk with a conversational partner about your experiences of that marginalization—thought, feelings, and images. Then, discuss the meaning of this incident to you. Next, discuss some of the effects of this marginalization on you and your relationships. Focus now on times when you were able to act outside its influence. How were you able to transcend these marginalizing stories? What possibilities might they offer you? Finally, how might this marginalization affect your work in understanding someone who might be in a more marginalized position? As a large group, discuss what contributed to your experience of marginalization. (This activity is adapted from Jill Freedman and Gene Combs, Evanston Family Therapy Center, Illinois.)

Epilogue: Future Storying of Spiritual Narratives

Narratively leading, teaching, worshipping, and caring join together in an understanding of liberative narrative ministry. It endeavors to find "unity through diversity" by recognizing the individual and collective expression of spiritual narratives with the witness of a faith community. The pastoral leader of a particular faith community seeks to be a storyteller of hope in which he or she does not abdicate responsibility but listens attentively to the stories that believers privilege for their own lives. The community becomes a witness to God's story for its own local expression while always reaching out to other communities to thicken spiritual narratives that sustain faith. It is to this style of ministry that we commit our passions and spirits.

Expansion of the practices outlined in this book may be a future direction that can thicken spiritual narratives. (See M. White, Narrative Practice: Continuing the Conversations for future directions of narrative.) The nonhierarchical approach of narrative ministry may also appeal to the new generation of believers in the emerging church. These persons experience "church" in a different, quite relational way (Merritt 2007).

Another narrative practice can be applied to community organizing. Historically, this practice has been seen as limited only to progressive liberal perspectives (Shannahan 2014). Sharing power with people links well with narrative therapy and liberation theology. In the future, we may be able to eliminate some of the difficult theological barriers and engage in genuine relationships that are transcendent.

Dulwich narrative practitioners interviewed Paulo Freire on April 24, 1997, the day before he died. He talked with passion about his interest in finding a way to rebuild people's wishes and desires—to create a "pedagogy of desire" (Veranda, Denborough and C. White, 1997). Our empowering and liberating God calls us to uncover and re-story our spiritual narrative so a faith of hope may be shared with a hurting world. This is my wish for future storying of liberative narrative ministry.

Appendix
Resources for Spiritual Narratives

KEY TERMS

- **Collective narrative ministry.** Narratively influenced ministry based on Denborough and Cheryl White's collective narrative practice, which emphasizes building unity with diversity, thus avoiding a false bifurcation between individual and group practices. Collective narrative ministry uses the re-storying of spiritual narratives through the collective practices of caring, leading, worshipping, and teaching.
- **Formative spiritual experience.** A spiritual experience that you know is true for you and serves as a source of strength.
- **Spiritual narrative.** Stories of faith that, over a period of time, extend into the future in ways that generate rich spiritual experiences, resulting in thickened faith for the believer.
- **Staff of Spirit.** A group spiritual practice that implements collective narrative methodology in a theological format influenced by liberation theology.

WEBSITES

- **Dulwich Centre** (www.dulwichcentre.com.au). Internationally focused website sponsored by the Dulwich Centre, co-founded by Michael and Cheryl White. The site includes a search engine linked to a comprehensive bibliography of narrative books and articles around the globe. Video podcasts are available from Friday Afternoons at Dulwich Centre (narrativetherapyonline.com) with a variety of presenters and topics.
- **Spiritual Narratives** (www.spiritualnarratives.com). This website, launched by this book's author, serves as a source for updates to this book. Resources include a blog, podcasts, PowerPoint and Prezi presentations, links, and the Staff of Spirit.

- **Narrative Approaches** (www.narrativeapproaches.com). David Epston's training events can be found on this website as well as other narrative training around the globe.
- **Narrative Therapy Online** (www.narrativetherapyonline.com). This goes directly to the video presentations of Friday Afternoons at Dulwich Centre on the Dulwich Center website. Persons can sign up to participate in this experience through postings.

Recommended Books

Bidwell, Duane. 2013. *Empowering Couples: A Narrative Approach to Spiritual Care*. Minneapolis: Fortress Press.

Coyle, Suzanne. 2013. *Re-storying Your Faith*. Winchester, UK: Circle Books.

Denborough, David. 2014. *Retelling the Stories of Our Lives: Everyday Narrative Therapy to Draw Inspiration and Transform Experience*. New York: W.W. Norton and Company.

Hester, Richard, and Kelli Walker-Jones. 2009. *Know Your Story and Lead with It: The Power of Narrative in Clergy Leadership*. Herndon, VA: Alban Institute.

Golemon, Larry, ed. 2010. *Finding Our Story: Narrative Leadership and Congregational Change*. Herndon, VA: Alban Institute.

____. 2010. *Living Our Story: Narrative Leadership and Congregational Culture*. Herndon, VA: Alban Institute.

____. 2010. *Teaching Our Story: Narrative Leadership and Pastoral Formation*. Herndon, VA: Alban Institute.

Neuger, Christie. 2001. *Counseling Women: A Narrative, Pastoral Approach*. Minneapolis: Fortress Press.

STAFF OF SPIRIT SPIRITUAL PRACTICE

The crook of the Staff of Spirit represents qualities of spirituality for the participant that are connected through relationships with self and others.[1] The cross on the Staff of Spirit represents qualities of spirituality relating to God through Jesus Christ. As participants use the Staff for telling their stories, their present spiritual experiences with significant others and God will be identified. Then, through telling and retelling with other group members functioning as outsider witnesses, the stories will be re-authored and doubly listened to. Stories of sustenance from the past can thus be used as a staff of strength for the future. A believer can choose a different staff for each journey. As a community of faith, we can also share our shepherd's staff with others on the journey. The Staff of Spirit is described as a way to develop storytelling into a spiritual practice that can enrich the participants' faith. Stories can be noted and reflected on in the future. Before beginning the process around the Staff of Spirit, participants are given the primary question the Staff invites: *What sustains you on your journey of faith?*

Participants are given a sheet with the Staff of Spirit logo on it so they can write down their stories and the stories of others, along with significant phrases for the outsider witness and definitional ceremony at the end of the process. With either silence or quiet music playing, each participant is asked to identify a formative spiritual experience to tell the other members of the group. A formative spiritual experience is defined as a spiritual experience that you know is true for you and serves as a source of strength. Taking turns, each participant tells the story of the formative spiritual experience to the group.

Spiritual Practice 1: Telling Your Spiritual Story

After telling the story, each participant is to write on the crook of the staff, beginning with the lower left quadrant, responses to the following questions:

- *What spiritual qualities does that story call forth in you?* (Lower left quadrant) This question is created to discover the absent but implicit. It is my experience that believers often miss those aspects or "spiritual qualities called forth" of their spiritual stories. It is *implicit* in Christian

1. The Staff of Spirit can be seen in color at www.spiritualnarratives.com. Colors on the Staff have some symbolic imagery from Christian traditions. The lower quadrant is green representing Jesus as liberator, giver of life and co-author of story; upper left quadrant purple representing spiritual repentance necessary for new stories; upper right quadrant brown representing place and social location of stories; and lower right quadrant red representing the sustenance of the Spirit.

faith to be meek and modest, not calling attention to those significant qualities that may nurture a spiritual story.

- *What other significant people have a relationship with you through these spiritual qualities?* (Upper left quadrant) This question is created to engage the participant in remembering people who relate with them through these spiritual qualities. Some people may no longer remain in relationship with those qualities while other new people may be admitted to the club of associations. This is also a question where histories of commitments can be explored.

- *What places and contexts do these spiritual qualities take you to?* (Upper right quadrant) This question focuses on the sometimes-ignored dimension of place in narrative practice. Recent literature focusing on place can give this question a firmer foundation. Spiritual experience is often focused within a place of worship or meditation. So, remembering can occur here both with people and places.

- *What spiritual qualities draw you closer to God?* (Lower right quadrant) This question reminds participants of God, who can be the ultimate "absent but implicit" even for believers. Many times explicit religious language can miss God, and implicit language and experience can draw God more vividly into the spiritual experience of the believer.

Participants in the four-week group are instructed to reflect daily, during their devotional time, on their story and written responses on the Staff of Spirit. Thoughts, prayers, phrases, biblical stories, and Bible passages that are evoked for them are to be written down and shared at the next meeting. Those who participate in the retreat are to do this practice after the completion of the retreat and then share with a fellow believer.

SPIRITUAL PRACTICE 2: RETELLING AND RESPONDING

Each participant retells a fellow believer's story of faith and the believer responds to his or her experience of that retelling.

The retelling of the story takes the form of outsider witnesses as each person responds to the story with four questions: What expressions of spirit caught your attention? What images do those spiritual expressions evoke? How do those spiritual expressions resonate with your own experiences? Where do those spiritual experiences transport you?

Some questions to be considered:

- *How has this spiritual story sustained you?* Responding to this question gives the participant an awareness of the effects of the spiritual story and so opens the person to future possibilities for re-storying the whole spiritual narrative.
- *How does this story call for the stories from Scripture?* The absent but implicit here lies in the ability of spiritual stories to reawaken stories from Scripture. In addition, this question invites the believer to notice resonances from other underlying stories.
- *What effects do these stories have on you now?* This question of relative influence can also open possibilities of relationships with the stories and the way in which people and places relating to the spiritual can be remembered.
- *What does the story call forth in you?* This question evokes the absent but implicit as well as the possibilities for re-authoring the story. Histories of skill and knowledge as well as of relationships may lie fallow but can be reawakened.

Participants serve as outsider witnesses to the story of each person who has shared the story.

Spiritual Practice 3: Spiritualities of the Everyday

Each participant is asked to meditate in silence or with music in the background. The facilitator will say: "You have shared a formative story of faith that has some sacred meaning. As we enter the world each day, we encounter many events and stories that may seem to have no connection with our spiritual story. Think of a challenge of just the past week and reflect on the following questions."

- *What qualities does it call forth from you?* (Write on the crook of the staff.) This is a beginning to re-authoring the dominant spiritual story by connecting the believer to everyday experience in a way similar to Michael White's "exoticizing the common." This explores the challenge of discovering the relationship of seemingly nonspiritual qualities to spiritual qualities that have been explicitly defined.

- *How did it move you to concerns that were bigger than you?* (Write on the cross of the staff.) This moves the believer to a re-authoring of those stories from explicitly spiritual as well as everyday experiences. A spiritual narrative focusing on ultimate meanings can emerge from these stories.
- *Who are you joined with in this challenge?* (Write those names on the staff.) Again, this question evokes remembering people from the past and present to further enrich the experience of double stories.

Participants share their written responses in the group and the other participants serve as outsider witnesses in the conversation.

SPIRITUAL PRACTICE 4: WITNESSING TO SPIRITUAL STORIES

All participants are asked to select a Staff of Spirit from another participant that would seem to sustain them through life challenges.

- *What stories on the Staff of Spirit most sustain you as you face challenges?* This question evokes the absent but implicit histories of knowledges and relationships that have supported and grown the sustaining stories of faith.
- *What are those challenges?* This question is reminiscent in some ways of Epston's backward story in that the questions in this exercise started on a positive note and now are inviting those challenges through an externalizing questions.
- *What qualities do you need for this challenge?* Through the question, the believer is drawn to a deeper level of double story in reflecting on what qualities are needed for this everyday challenge. He or she can reflect on ways in which those qualities call forth histories of knowledges and relationships that can be woven in the re-authored story.

CONSENT FORM

Christian Theological Seminary
Informed Consent for Participants
in Research Projects Involving Human Subjects

Title of Project: <u>Storytelling as Spiritual Practice</u>

Principle Investigator: <u>Suzanne Coyle, Ph.D.</u>

1. <u>Purpose of Research</u>

The purpose of this study is to explore the effectiveness of a collective narrative practice on the ability of participants to restory their faith story as it relates to everyday life.

1. <u>Procedures</u>

Your participation in this study is completely voluntary. If you wish to discontinue your participation in this study at any time, you may do so without facing any adverse consequences. You will be asked to participate in a group process using a spiritual assessment instrument called the Staff of Spirit. At the conclusion of the group, you will be asked to an evaluation form.

1. <u>Risks</u>

Risks of participating in this program are minimal. As a result of the group discussions, some emotional distress may occur for you.

1. <u>Benefits</u>

Participation in this group may help you deepen your faith stories and as a result contribute to your spiritual growth. In addition, the results of this study will contribute to the narrative practice and pastoral theology literature and thus may help other people in the life of the church.

1. <u>Extent of Anonymity and Confidentiality</u>

Strict confidentiality of information will be preserved. This means that we won't tell anyone what you say in the questionnaires. You will be assigned an identification number that will be kept separate from any identifying information, and your questionnaires will contain only this identification number. Names will not be used on any reports or publications that are developed from the results of this study.

1. Compensation

There will be no compensation for participation in this study.

1. Freedom to Withdraw

You do not have to participate in this research study. If you agree to participate, you can withdraw your participation at any time without penalty.

1. Participant's Responsibilities

I voluntarily agree to participate in this study. I have the following responsibilities:
1. I will complete a questionnaire before beginning the group to the best of my ability.
2. I will attend four group sessions or one-day retreat and participate as I am able and willing.
3. I will complete a questionnaire upon completion of the group to the best of my ability.
4. I can attest that I do not currently have Dr. Coyle as a professor or supervisor.

1. Participant's Permission

I have read the Consent Form and conditions of this project. I have had all my questions answered. I hereby acknowledge the above and give my voluntary consent.

Participant's Signature   Date

Participant's Name (please print)

Researcher's Signature   Date

Sample Syllabi with Narrative Methodology

Sample syllabi are included to serve as possible templates for, first, a cultural immersion experience and, second, a class on narrative ministry.

The first syllabus can be used as an example for a congregational cultural immersion experience or a seminary cross cultural immersion course with this methodology.

The second syllabus is a template for a seminary course focusing on "Narrative Ministry" that would fit in Christian ministry or pastoral care classes. The optimal pedagogy would involve a teaching team representing the Christian ministry and pastoral care fields. With this teaching style, the pastoral care faculty person would be the course instructor rotating with lecture and discussion from other faculty representing preaching, leadership, and Christian education.

X-730 1—Mountain Stories: Re-storying Spiritual Narratives

Cross-Cultural Immersion Course
Appalachian Ministries Resource Center

Sponsored by
Christian Theological Seminary
Project Director—Rev. Suzanne Coyle, Ph.D., LMFT
Mentors—Rev. Lon Oliver, D.Min.; Rev. Ben Pogue
May 14–May 25, 2012

Course Description

This course is a cultural immersion course in eastern Kentucky. This course will focus on written and oral Appalachian stories as a basis for instilling confidence in self and community through a narrative-based model of pastoral care. Robert Schenkkan's *The Kentucky Cycle* will be analyzed to explore the history and images of life in eastern Kentucky. Through reading and visits with storytellers, we will look at the lives of contemporary authors through narrative theology and interpret liberation theology in the Appalachian context.

GOAL OF COURSE

The goal of this course is to lift up indigenous mountain stories, both oral and written, as a model for pastoral care to individuals, families, and communities in need of a liberating spirit.

LEARNING METHODOLOGY

Students will immerse themselves in the culture of eastern Kentucky primarily through meeting the people and places of Appalachia. Learning will first focus on the stories of the participants in the class while they use narrative therapy as a means to accomplish this goal.

Then, with narrative work as a basis, students will discuss *The Kentucky Cycle* and respond to this work throughout the course to determine its relative reality or unreality. The course will then unfold to examine the life and work of James Still and George Ella Lyon as each writer presents his or her own personal story intertwined with the story of the region.

Students will engage in action research as they interview members of a selected congregation regarding their personal spiritual narratives through a collective narrative process called "Staff of Spirit," which was created by the instructor. This process uses storytelling as spiritual practice. Students will have opportunity to participate and facilitate in this spiritual practice as well as to interview members of the congregation and worship with them.

Storyteller Randy Wilson will engage the group as we begin to integrate narrative and liberation theology to create a model of pastoral care based on the action research. Interspersed in this course will be an introduction to the role of African American stories in Appalachia as well as a visit to Appalshop.

Each day will end with a time for personal and community reflection. Required readings are best read before the course begins. You may read some during the class travels. Please read the books by Still and Lyon prior to the course. Students will keep a daily journal as well as develop a final project due after completion of the immersion experience.

Some technology may be used to enhance learning as available.

STUDENT LEARNING OUTCOMES

- To experience life in Appalachia in an immersion setting
- To learn narrative approaches to pastoral care through reading and exercises

- To integrate narrative therapy and liberation theology as a resources for pastoral care
- To engage in action research with residents of Appalachia

EVALUATION

Students will complete an evaluation form about the course at its conclusion. The professor will invite feedback during the course and make any helpful changes during the course to maximize the students' learning.

GRADES

Grades will be assigned according to the grading scale of Christian Theological Seminary and then converted as the student's seminary may request. Christian Theological Seminary Grading Scale: A, A-, B , B, B-, C , C, C-, D , D, D-, F.

REQUIRED READING

Brown, Robert McAfee. 1993. *Liberation Theology: An Introductory Guide.* Louisville, KY: Westminster/John Knox.

Denborough, David. 2008. *Collective Narrative Practice: Responding to Individuals, Groups and Communities Who Have Experienced Trauma.* Adelaide, South Australia: Dulwich Centre Publications.

Schenkkan, Robert. 1998. *The Kentucky Cycle.* New York: Dramatist's Play Service.

Lyon, George Ella. 2007. *With a Hammer for My Heart: A Novel.* Lexington, KY: University Press of Kentucky.

Still, James. 1991. *The Wolfpen Notebooks: A Record of Appalachian Life.* Lexington, KY: University Press of Kentucky.

WRITTEN ASSIGNMENTS

Personal journal. Students will write a daily entry that reflects their struggles with processing what they experience with their own personal story. Use a small spiral-bound notebook. Due May 25.

Integrative paper. Students will write an integrative paper weaving narrative therapy, liberation theology, and either an oral or written Appalachian story that challenges the way the student lives in his or her own cultural context. Due June 25.

GROUP PROJECT

The professor will engage in action research about spiritual narratives and may collaborate with the professor in writing a monograph that integrates the learning and action research of the group in creating an inductive model of pastoral care based on spiritual narratives. An attempt will be made to publish the results in written or video format for distribution to the pastoral theological guild and the narrative therapy community. Students' contributions will be cited in the document. This portion of the immersion course will not be graded.

TENTATIVE SESSION SCHEDULE

Precourse
Read as much of the assigned readings as possible in the following order: Lyon, Still, Schenkkan, Denborough, and Brown.

Course
May 14 (Monday)—Berea:
Morning—Gathering and orientation by Lon Oliver and Suzanne Coyle
LUNCH at AMERC office
Afternoon—Tour of arts and crafts community; visit with Mary Comer, storyteller and doll maker
DINNER—Boone Tavern
LODGING in Berea

May 15 (Tuesday)—Berea:
Morning—Appalachia and the African American experience with Dr. William Turner of Berea College
LUNCH
Afternoon—Narratives of the writer George Ella Lyon
DINNER
Evening—Northern family
LODGING in Berea

May 16 (Wednesday)—Berea:
Morning—Affrilachian poets—Bianca Spriggs—hopefully Berea maybe Lexington
LUNCH
Afternoon—Travel to CleftRock

DINNER—CleftRock
LODGING—CleftRock

May 17 (Thursday)—CleftRock:
Retreat

May 18 (Friday)—CleftRock:
Retreat

May 19 (Saturday)—CleftRock:
Congregational interviews

May 20 (Sunday)—Appalachian Congregation:
Lead a group of laity in Staff of Spirit process designed to re-story spiritual faith at a selected Kentucky congregation. Lodging Saturday evening at town of congregation. Attend worship at church on Sunday.

May 21 (Monday)—Hindman:
Visit Hindman Settlement School
Storytelling with Randy Wilson
LODGING—Hindman

May 22 (Tuesday)—Whitesburg:
Visit Apalshop—Darryl Mullins
View *Stranger with a Camera*
LODGING—Whitesburg or CleftRock

May 23 (Wednesday)—Travel back to CleftRock:
Possible mountaintop removal experience
Retreat

May 24 (Thursday)—CleftRock:
Retreat

May 25 (Friday)—CleftRock:
Retreat

Narrative Ministry Syllabus

Purpose of Course

Narrative Ministry is designed to implement theory of narrative therapy as co-developed by White and Epston and other narrative approaches in a multistoried view of pastoral care, preaching/worship, administration, Christian education, and community outreach. Students will learn the theory of narratives practices and ways to implement them in ministry.

Student Learning Outcomes

Students will achieve the following student learning outcomes, based on the standards of the Association for Theological Schools:

ATS Educational Standards
A.2.3 Cultural Context
A.2.3.1—Students will understand cultural and social issues of ministry.

A.2.4 Personal and Spiritual Formation
A.2.4.1—Students will understand ministerial roles and ways to practice them.
A.2.4.2—Students will learn ways to be committed to Christian faith and life.

A.2.5–Capacity for Ministry and Public Leadership
A.2.5.1—Students will learn ways to integrate relationships between ministry approaches and theory.
A.2.5.3—Students will have opportunity for practice in a supervised ministry setting.

Method

The course will use collaborative learning through team teaching by faculty and peer learning with other students. Didactic lectures will be supplemented by PowerPoint and Prezi presentations, films, music, student presentations, guest speakers, Skype visitors, and spiritual formation groups.

Assignments

- *Personal spiritual formation.* Students will keep recordings of spiritual practice according to the narratively informed *Re-storying Your Faith* spiritual practice guide.

SLOs: A.2.4.2.

Graded: P/F

- *Spiritual formation group.* Students will participate in a Staff of Spirit spiritual practice as described in *Uncovering Spiritual Narratives.* Faculty will assign students to groups with diversity of gender and racial ethnicity as class enrollment allows.

SLOs: A.2.4.2

Graded: P/F

- *Reflection questions.* Students will be responsible as assigned for creating reflection questions for class discussion.

SLOs: A.2.5.1

Graded: Letter grade

- *Narrative ministry practice.* Students will create a narrative ministry practice for use in their field education experience according to *Uncovering Spiritual Narratives* and *Collective Narrative Practice.* The narrative practice must include five of the ten narrative principles in *Collective Narrative Practice.* The paper, including theory and practice, will not exceed twenty-five pages in a quality and format suitable for publication.

SLOs: A.2.3.1., A.2.4.1, A.2.5.1, A.2.5.3

Graded: Letter grade

Texts

Primary Text

Coyle, Suzanne. 2014. *Uncovering Spiritual Narratives: Using Story in Pastoral Care and Ministry.* Minneapolis: Fortress Press.

Required Texts

Coyle, Suzanne. 2013. *Re-storying Your Faith.* Winchester, UK: Circle Books.

Denborough, David. 2008. *Collective Narrative Practice: Responding to Individuals, Groups, and Communities Who Have Experienced Trauma.* Adelaide, South Australia: Dulwich Centre Publications.

Denborough, David. 2014. *Retelling the Stories of Our Lives: Everyday Narrative Therapy to Draw Inspiration and Transform Experience.* New York: W. W. Norton.

Hester, Richard Hester, and Kelli Walker-Jones. 2009. *Know Your Story and Lead with It: The Power of Narrative in Clergy Leadership.* Herndon, VA: Alban Institute.

Golemon, Larry, ed. 2010. *Finding Our Story: Narrative Leadership and Congregational Change.* Herndon, VA: Alban Institute.

Golemon, Larry, ed. 2010. *Living Our Story: Narrative Leadership and Congregational Culture.* Herndon, VA: Alban Institute.

Golemon, Larry, ed. 2010. *Teaching Our Story: Narrative Leadership and Pastoral Formation.* Herndon, VA: Alban Institute.

Morgan, Alice. 2000. *Narrative Therapy: An Easy to Read Introduction.* Adelaide, South Australia: Dulwich Centre Publications.

CLASS SESSIONS

Narrative practice asks questions to generate experiences for potential new stories. So, each class poses a question.

UNDERSTANDING NARRATIVE MINISTRY

Class 1—What Is Collective Narrative Practice?
Readings: Morgan, *Narrative Therapy*

Class 2—What Is Narrative Practice?
Readings: Denborough, *Collective Narrative Practice*; Morgan, *NT*

Class 3—Who Tells the Story?
Readings: Coyle, *Spiritual Narratives*, ch. 1; Denborough, *CNP*; Denborough, *Everyday Narrative*; Hester and Walker-Jones, *Know Your Story*

PRACTICING NARRATIVE MINISTRY

Class 4—How Are We Formed Narratively?

Readings: Coyle, *Re-storying Your Faith*; Denborough, *EN*; Hester and Walker-Jones, *KYS*

Class 5—How Do We Voice Narrative Ministry?
Readings: Coyle, *SN*, ch. 2; Golemon

Class 6—How Do We Voice Narrative Ministry?
Readings: Coyle, *SN*; Golemon

Class 7—How Do We Narratively Care?
Readings—Coyle, *SN*, ch. 3; Golemon

Class 8—How Do We Narratively Lead?
Readings—Coyle, *SN*, ch. 4; Golemon

Class 9—How Do We Narratively Worship?
Readings—Coyle, *SN*, ch. 4; Golemon

Class 10—How Do We Narratively Teach?
Readings—Coyle, *SN*, ch. 4; Golemon
Extending Narrative Ministry

Class 11—How Does Narrative Ministry Practice Spirituality?
Readings: Coyle, *SN*, ch. 5; Coyle, *RYF*

Class 12—What Does Narrative Ministry Say to Social Justice?
Readings: Coyle, SN, ch. 6; Golemon

*Classes 13 & 14—*Student Presentations

References

Akinyela, Makungu. 2002. "De-colonizing Our Lives: Divining a Post-Colonial Therapy." *International Journal of Narrative Therapy and Community Work* 2: 32–43.

Allen, Ron. E-mail, September 27, 2013.

Allen, Ron. 2008. *Preaching and the Other: Studies of Postmodern Insights.* St. Louis: Chalice.

Barker, Kim. 2009. "Opening a Crack: An Account of Narrative Practice in the Context of Pastoral Theology." *International Journal of Narrative Therapy and Community Work* 1:48–59.

Bidwell, Duane. 2013. *Empowering Couples: A Narrative Approach to Spiritual Care.* Minneapolis: Fortress Press.

Boff, Leonardo. 1987. *The Maternal Face of God: The Feminine and Its Religious Expression.* New York: Collins Publications.

Boff, Leonardo, and Clodovis Boff. 1987. *Introducing Liberation Theology.* Trans. Paul Burns. Maryknoll, NY: Orbis.

Boulton, Matthew. 2013. "Much Ado about 'Nones.'" Salt and Light. Blog post, January 13. http://www.thesaltandlightblog.com/?p=393.

Bruner, Jerome. 1987a. *Actual Minds, Possible Worlds.* Cambridge, MA: Harvard University Press.

____. 1987b. "Life as Narrative." *Social Research* 54 (1): 11–32.

Capps, Donald. 1998. *Living Stories: Pastoral Counseling in Congregational Context.* Minneapolis: Fortress Press.

Conde-Frazier, Elizabeth. 2004. "The Holy Spirit." In *Handbook of U.S. Theologies of Liberation,* ed. Miguel De La Torre. St. Louis: Chalice.

Congar, Yves. 1983a. *Called to Life.* Danvers, MA: Crossroad.

____. 1983b. "Motherhood in God and the Femininity of the Holy Spirit." In *I Believe in the Holy Spirit.* New York: Seabury Press.

Coyle, Suzanne. 2007. "The Bible, Pastoral Care, and Conversational Practices." In *Text and Community: Essays in Memory of Bruce Metzger,* ed. J. Harold Ellens. Sheffield, UK: Sheffield Phoenix.

____. 2010. "Spiritual Narratives: Hope and Healing through Stories of Faith." In *Healing Power of Religion: How Faith Helps Humans Thrive*, ed. J. Harold Ellens. Santa Barbara, CA: Praeger.

____. 2011a. "Appalachian Narratives, Cultural Discourses, and Theological Witness." *Encounter* 72 (1): 125–32.

____. 2011b. "Storytelling as Spiritual Practice: Staff of Spirit." Unpublished paper for International Training Program in Narrative Therapy and Community Practice at Dulwich Centre, Adelaide, South Australia.

____. 2013. *Re-storying Your Faith*. Winchester, UK: Circle Books.

____. In press. "Many Members, Many Stories: Moving from Family Systems to Family Narratives." In *Transforming Wisdom: Pastoral Psychotherapy in Theological Perspective*, ed. Felicity Kelcourse and Bernie Lyon. Eugene, OR: Cascade Books.

Craddock, Fred. 2008. "Story, Narrative, and Metanarrative." In *What's the Shape of Narrative Preaching?*, ed. Mike Graves and David Schlafer. St. Louis: Chalice.

Daniel, Lillian. 2006. *Tell It Like It Is: Reclaiming the Practice of Testimony*. Herndon: Alban Institute.

De La Torre, Miguel. 2004. *Doing Christian Ethics from the Margins*. Maryknoll, NY: Orbis.

Denborough, David. 2008. *Collective Narrative Practices: Responding to Individuals, Groups, and Communities Who Have Experienced Trauma*. Adelaide, South Australia: Dulwich Centre Publications.

____. 2014. *Retelling the Stories of Our Lives: Everyday Narrative Therapy to Draw Inspiration and Transform Experience*. New York: W. W. Norton and Company.

Doehring, Carrie. 2006. *The Practice of Pastoral Care: A Postmodern Approach*. Louisville, KY: Westminster John Knox.

Duvall, Jim, and Laura Béres. 2013. *Innovations in Narrative Therapy: Connecting Practice, Training, and Research*. New York: W. W. Norton.

Dyskstra, Robert. 2005. *Images of Pastoral Care: Classic Readings*. St. Louis: Chalice.

Epston, David. 2010. Conversation, in Adelaide, South Australia.

____. December 2010. *International Narrative Therapy and Community Work Training*. Dulwich Centre, Adelaide, South Australia.

____. 2013. "The Craft and Art of Narrative Therapy Enquiry." Workshop sponsored by the Evanston Family Therapy Center. June 25–26.

Epston, David, and Michael White. 1992. *Experience, Contradiction, Narrative and Imagination: Selected Papers of David Epston and Michael White 1989–1991.* Adelaide, South Australia: Dulwich Centre Publications.

Fairfax, Kayte. 1995. "Urban Public Places as Men's Places? The Role of Public Transport in Enabling Women to Reclaim Our Urban Environment After Dark." Unpublished honors dissertation, Department of Geography, Victoria University of Wellington, NZ.

Foucault, Michel.1984. "Space, Knowledge, and Power." In *The Foucault Reader*, ed. P. Rabinow, 239–56. London: Penguin.

Freedman, Jill. 2010. "Narrative Therapy" Lecture presented at the Toronto International Summer School of Narrative Practice Toronto, Canada. July 7–9.

Freedman, Jill, and Gene Combs. 1996. *Narrative Therapy: The Social Construction of Preferred Realities.* New York: W. W. Norton.

Freire, Paulo. 1986. *Pedagogy of the Oppressed.* New York: Continuum.

____. 1994. *Pedagogy of Hope: Reliving Pedagogy of the Oppressed.* New York: Bloomsbury Academics.

____. 1997. *Pedagogy of the Heart.* New York: Continuum.

Friedman, Edwin. 1985. *Generation to Generation: Family Process in Church and Synagogue.* New York: Guilford Press.

Geertz, Clifford. 1973. *Interpretation of Culture.* New York: Basic Books.

____. 1983. *Local Knowledge.* New York: Basic Books.

Golemon, Larry. 2010a. "The Practice of Narrative Leadership in Ministry." In *Living Our Story: Narrative Leadership and Congregational Culture*, ed. Larry Golemon. Herndon, VA: Alban Institute.

____. 2010b. "Thinking through Change: Narrative Theory and Models of Transformation." In *Finding Our Story: Narrative Leadership and Congregational Change*, ed. Larry Golemon. Herndon, VA: Alban Institute.

____. 2010c. "Toward a Framework for Narrative Leadership in Ministry." In *Teaching Our Story: Narrative Leadership and Pastoral Formation*, ed. Larry Golemon. Herndon, VA: Alban Institute.

Grey, Mary. 1991. "Where Does the Wild Goose Fly To: Seeking a New Theology of Spirit for Feminist Theology." *New Black Friars* 72 (846): 89–96.

Griffith, James, and Melissa Griffith. 2003. *Encountering the Sacred in Psychotherapy: How to Talk with People about Their Spiritual Lives.* New York: Guilford.

Hauerwas, Stanley. 1981. *The Community of Character*. Notre Dame, IN: University of Notre Dame Press.

Hester, Richard, and Kelli Walker-Jones. 2009. *Know Your Story and Lead with It: The Power of Narrative in Clergy Leadership*. Herndon, VA: Alban Institute.

Hiltner, Seward. 1958. *Preface to Pastoral Theology*. Nashville, TN: Abingdon.

Hodge, David. 2005. "Spiritual Life Maps: A Client-Centered Pictorial Instrument for Spiritual Assessment, Planning, and Intervention." *Social Work* 50 (1): 77–87.

Hoffman, Kathyn. 2010. *Shared Narrative: Story Brokering as an Approach to Contextual Learning at Seminary*. Herndon, VA: Alban Institute.

Lester, Andrew. 1995. *Hope in Pastoral Care and Counseling*. Louisville, KY: Westminster John Knox.

Lester, Jane. 2001. "Family Equals People, Land and Language." In *Telling Our Stories in Ways That Make Us Stronger*, ed. B. Wingard and J. Lester, 57–62. Adelaide, South Australia: Dulwich Centre Publications.

Madigan, Stephen. 2011. *Narrative Therapy*. Washington, DC: APA Press.

Merritt, Carol. 2007. *Tribal Church: Ministering to the Missing Generation*. Herndon, VA: Alban Institute.

Meteyard, John. 2008. "Narrative Therapy and Narrative Theology: A Conversation." In *Interweavings: Conversations between Narrative Therapy and Christian Faith*, ed. Richard Cook and Irene Alexander. North Charleston, SC: Create Space Books.

Miller-McLemore, Bonnie. 2012. *Christian Theology in Practice*. Grand Rapids: William B. Eerdmans Publishing Company.

Moschella, Mary Clark. 2008. *Ethnography as a Pastoral Practice: An Introduction*. Cleveland: Pilgrim.

Mucherera, Tapiwa. 2009. *Meet Me at the Palaver: Narrative Pastoral Counseling in Postcolonial Contexts*. Eugene, OR: Cascade.

"Narativ 2-Day Listening and Storytelling Workshop for Helping Professionals," November 8 and 9, 2013, New York, New York.

Narativ Inc. 2013. "Narativ 2-Day Listening and Storytelling Workshop for Helping Professionals" Handbook. New York: Narativ Inc.

"Narrative Therapy Charter of Story-Telling Rights." Accessed on April 1, 2013. http://www.dulwichcentre.com.au/current-projects.html.

Neuger, Christie. 2001. *Counseling Women: A Narrative Pastoral Approach*. Minneapolis: Fortress Press.

Payne, Martin. 2006. *Narrative Therapy: An Introduction for Counsellors*. London: Sage.

Poling, James. 2011. *Rethinking Faith: A Constructive Practical Theology.* Minneapolis: Fortress Press.

Raheim, Salome, Maggie Carey, Charles Waldegrave, Kiwi Tamansese, Flora Tuhaka, Hugh Fox, Anita Franklin, Cheryl White, and David Denborough. n.d. *An Invitation to Narrative Practitioners to Address Privilege and Dominance.* Accessed on April 1, 2013. http://www.dulwichcentre.com.au/privilege.html.

Ricoeur, Paul. 1984. *Time and Narrative.* Vol. 3. Chicago: University of Chicago Press.

Savage, Carl, and William Presnell. 2008. *Narrative Research in Ministry: A Postmodern Research Approach for Faith Communities.* Louisville, KY: Wayne Oates Institute.

Scalise, Charles. 2003. *Bridging the Gap: Connecting What You Learned in Seminary with What You Find in the Congregation.* Nashville, TN: Abingdon.

Shannahan, Chris. 2014. *A Theology of Community Organizing: Power to the People.* New York: Routledge.

Shapiro, Tim. 2010. "The Sacred Value of Congregational Stories." In *Living Our Story: Narrative Leadership and Congregational Culture,* ed. Larry Golemon. Herndon, VA: Alban Institute.

Thomas, Frank.1997. *They Like to Never Quite Praisin' God: The Role of Celebration in Preaching.* Cleveland: United Church Press.

Townsend, Loren. 2009. *Introduction to Pastoral Counseling.* Nashville: Abingdon Press.

Trudinger, Mark. 2006. "Maps of Violence, Maps of Hope: Using Place and Maps to Explore Identity, Gender, and Violence." *International Journal of Narrative Therapy and Community Work* 3:11–42.

Veranda, Walter, David Denborough, and Cheryl White. "Making History and Unveiling Oppression: An Interview with Paulo Freire," April 24, 1997.

Vygotsky, Lev. 1986. *Thought and Language.* Cambridge, MA: MIT Press.

Waldegrave, Charles, Kiwi Tamasese, Flora Tuhaka, and Warihi Cambell. 2004. *Just Therapy—a Journey: A Collection of Papers from the Just Therapy Team.* Adelaide, South Australia: Dulwich Centre Publications.

White, Cheryl. 2008. "Introduction." *International Journal of Narrative Therapy and Community Work* 1: 35–26.

White, Michael. Spring, 1988. "Saying Hullo Again: The Incorporation of the Lost Relationship in the Resolution of Grief." *Dulwich Centre Newsletter,* 7-11.

_____. 1995. *Re-Authoring Lives: Interviews and Essays.* Adelaide, South Australia: Dulwich Centre Publications.

_____. 1997. *Narratives of Therapists' Lives.* Adelaide, South Australia: Dulwich Centre Publications.

_____. 2000a. "Re-engaging with History: The Absent but Implicit." In *Reflections on Narrative Practice: Essays and Interviews.* Adelaide, South Australia: Dulwich Centre Publications.

_____. 2000b. *Reflections on Narrative Practice: Essays and Interviews.* Adelaide, South Australia: Dulwich Centre Publications.

_____. 2004. *Narrative Practice and Exotic Lives: Resurrecting Diversity in Everyday Lives.* Adelaide, South Australia: Dulwich Centre Publications.

_____. 2005. "Workshop Notes." Dulwich Centre. September 21. http://www.dulwichcentre.com.au/michael-white-workshop-notes.pdf.

_____. 2007. *Maps of Narrative Practice.* New York: W.W. Norton.

_____2011. Narrative Practice: Continuing the Conversations. New York: W.W. Norton and Company.

White, Michael, Michael Hoyt, and Gene Combs. 1995. "On Ethics and the Spiritualities of the Surface." In *Constructive Therapies*, vol. 2, ed. Michael Hoyt. New York: Continuum.

Williams, Daniel Day. 1970. *The Spirit and the Forms of Love.* New York: Harper and Row.

Wimberly, Edward. 1997. *Recalling Our Own Stories: Spiritual Renewal for Religious Caregivers.* San Francisco: John Wiley.

CPSIA information can be obtained
at www.ICGtesting.com
Printed in the USA
LVOW01s0756041115
461058LV00012B/151/P